Grevilles telegram company

Mediums and their dupes

Grevilles telegram company

Mediums and their dupes

ISBN/EAN: 9783742858962

Manufactured in Europe, USA, Canada, Australia, Japa

Cover: Foto ©Thomas Meinert / pixelio.de

Manufactured and distributed by brebook publishing software
(www.brebook.com)

Grevilles telegram company

Mediums and their dupes

PREFACE.

——:o:——

THIS pamphlet is published by the several authors of the different papers, not for the sake of profit nor gain, but from a higher motive. They, as honest recorders of events and public critics, each from their own different point of view, have taken up pen to expose and lash one of the greatest impostures of modern times which during the last few years has acquired such firm hold on many dupes in Australia. The authors claim the support and sympathy of all Christian and sober-minded citizens in their endeavours to frustrate the designs of the professional mediums whose fraudulent machinations have unseated the faith of hundreds and have sapped the foundations of Religion, Morality, and Social Order.

SYDNEY, MARCH, 1879.

THE WORLD OF DUPES.

——o——

Robert G. Ingersoll has well said primal man "dwelt in an unreal world. He mistook his ideas, his dreams for real things. His fears became terrible and malicious monsters. He lived in the midst of fairies and furies, nymphs and naiads, goblins and ghosts, witches and wizards, spirits and spooks, deities and devils The obscure and gloomy depths were filled with claw and wing, with beak and hoof, with leering looks and sneering mouths, with the malice of deformity, with the cunning of hatred, and with all the slimy forms that fear can draw and paint upon the shadowy canvas of the dark." The God of primal man has ever been a malignant spirit ready to devour his human children unless propitiated by costly offerings and terrible sacrifices. Amongst all people and through all ages certain cunning mortals have endowed themselves with supernatural and magical powers trading on the fears of the majority,—their dupes. "Medicine men," sorcerers, and "Obi-men" manufacture charms and perform incantations and are handsomely rewarded for the exercise of the powers over the spirits of good or evil fortune which they alone are supposed to possess. One extraordinary fact shows how the world is and has ever been duped. The gods or spirits never work for nothing. The priests of Baal, of Jove or Apollo, of Isis and Osiris, of Vishnu and Siva, these the representatives of the highest form of intellectual superstition have always been on a par with the medicine man of the Red Indian, or sorcerer of the South Seas, in that, if anything special was required from the deity whose acts they claimed to influence, they themselves had first to be directly paid, or indirectly through offerings being made to the God who was appealed to.

In civilized communities we have changed all this, Christianity and Science have swept away the cobwebs of superstition. We have gauged the forces of Nature and fear them not. The Catholic Church it is true still claims for its priests certain powers, and peculiar virtues are still supposed to hang around the relics of the saints. A new miracle has been invented in the apparition of Our Lady of Lourdes, and the excursion trains carrying the Pilgrims to her shrine have greatly benefited the French railroads. But the Catholic priest derives his power only from the church and does not claim any *personal* attributes. Except amongst the most ignorant or savage races, sorcerers, witches, and wizards are things of the past. This is in truth an Age of Unbelief. To the educated, science demonstrates everything. By "evolution" we are what we are. In a few millions of years we shall be diffused by some regular process of nature, and

the atoms of our world will help to form another, and it is to be hoped
a better one. Thus science! To the ignorant, except those who
remain bound to the Catholic Church, infidelity has been arrived at by
many causes; but all over the world, in America, England, and in
most countries on the Continent, amongst the masses scepticism
increases, and there is not the same implicit belief in the old faiths.
That they are in any way worse than their equals in former ages I
a n not prepared to admit.

They have forsaken the Gods of their fathers! They believe not
the teaching of the Churches! Yet amongst many there is still a
fear, a dread of, or a curiosity concerning the unknown. There may
be an "undiscovered country." And many have also fond yearnings
to meet again in the spirit the loved ones who have gone before.
The churches with their cold dogmas satisfy them not. Each man
wishes a sign for himself, and so in this enlightened sceptical
nineteenth century with steam and electricity and phonographs and
telephones, the reductio ad absurdum of superstition and gullibility has
been arrived at. The world is still full of ready dupes, and the
medicine men and sorcerers of the savage who sell you protecting
charms, or will perform some mummery supposed to make you lucky
in the war or chase, for a moderate sum payable in the currency of the
country, have their equals in the "spiritualistic mediums" who for
half a guinea will rap you out a communication from the unseen
world. It is the same old fraud! Certain individuals pretend to be
alone endued with faculties of communication and powers over the
unknown, which they exercise for the benefit of their dupes and for
dollars No cash, no show!

The "spirit rapping" mania sprung up about a quarter of a
century ago. This with "table turning" has been a source of
amusement in many private families. I have been present at domestic
seances and I have seen things I cannot account for. But certainly I
never gave "the spirits" credit for their manifestations Rather I
attributed them to the unconscious deception (of which Dr. Knaggs
speaks further on) of some members of the circle. I admit that there
may be some "force" within ourselves which is not yet properly
understood. But it is not with the parlour phase of spiritualism that
I now deal. It is with those professional impostors who trade on our
weakness. They have evolved the most ludicrous surroundings to their
manifestations. The spirits it appears take delight in the silliest of
puerile means to demonstrate their presence to mortals, and they
generally require a darkened room in which to perform third-rate
conjurors' tricks. Some fifteen years ago the Davenport Brothers
commenced their career with the celebrated rope tying business.
They have been exposed time after time yet still found dupes to
believe in them, and two years back when in Melbourne were claimed
by the Banner of Light as true mediums. The Davenports first
introduced the cabinet, as inside that they were free from scrutiny.
Thus what believers think adds to the wonder of the "manifestations" is in reality quite otherwise. These jugglers first evolved the

"spirit hand" which in a darkened room appeared at the edge of a table. This it was discovered was only a stuffed glove attached to the boot of one of the Brothers. The rope tying trick is now done by many clever professional conjurors, and in a manner superior to the Davenport's.

Some new trick was required to gull the world of dupes and the latest outcome of imposture is the slate writing business, the chief exponent of which is now in the colonies. "Dr." Henry Slade is a charlatan and rogue of the first water. Recent proceedings of his which have come to my knowledge prove him to be a dangerous cunning villain who deserves to be lashed naked through the world. In the following articles his trickery as exhibited here is fully exposed. But let us first see what is his record in the old world. I know nothing of the earlier career of this arch-impostor who has found so many ready dupes here. But in 1876 "Dr." Henry Slade made his appearance in London, and fools flocked to hear him and paid their sovereigns to communicate with the spirits of the dead through the agency of a table, a slate, and a pencil. Slade however was very cautious at this time and unless he perceived a dupe who would swallow everything "the spirits" said, deceased relatives would not always give "manifestations." But as his clients must have something for their money he evolved the spirit of a presumed departed wife with whom he held affectionate intercourse, and who gave general but vague information as to affairs in spirit land Slade at this time had an accomplice, one Simmons. Dupes and sovereigns multiplied, and the impostors would still perchance be piling up their wealth in the Modern Babylon, but that certain sceptics belonging to the varied walks of science, literature, and the stage (as is the case in the production of this pamphlet,) each working from their own point of view at last succeeded in fully exposing the fraudulent *modus operandi* of the "medium."

On October 2nd, 1876, Henry Slade was charged at Bow-street Police Court, before Mr. Flowers, with obtaining money under false pretences. The case lasted for more than three weeks, and created much excitement in the minds of the spiritualists. The chief witnesses were the well known novelist, Mrs. Ross Church (daughter of Captain Marryatt), Miss Kate Field of New York, Professor Lankester, Doctors Donkin and Carpenter, and Mr. Maskelyne, the celebrated "conjuror" of the Egyptian Hall. The evidence as to Slade's performances, proves that they were exactly of the same character as those with which he has been lately treating the dupes of Sydney in Wynyard Square. None of the witnesses however appear to have had the ingenious inspiration of Dr. Knaggs in seeing what Slade did underneath the table by the aid of a mirror. The table used in London was exactly the same as that in Australia, "an ordinary kitchen table about four feet square. It had the ordinary frame work around the central portion of the table and the legs, to the depth of six or eight inches, outside which the flaps projected." Mr Maskelyne's evidence was most interesting. Of the slate writing he says, "It is a very good trick and the point is this. It seem impossible that a man with a heavy slate can hold it and produce writing with the same fingers beneath the slate. It is however very easy, especially if there is a cross piece, as in the table in court, to push the slate against it and help to support it. The slate can then be supported by the thumb, and the whole of the fingers left at liberty. The best way of holding the pencil is, not under the finger nail for that is impracticable, but by an apparatus like this (producing a little thimble with attached pencil, fastened by elastic beneath his sleeve, which disappeared of itself when let go.) With this instantaneously fixed on the end of his finger he held the slate before him with the left hand, and resting the thumb of the right hand on one side and having the fingers loose on the other, rapidly wrote a few words, which, when the slate was handed up to the bench, Mr. Flowers read amidst great laughter, thus. ' *The Spirits are present.*' "

Mr. Maskelyne went on to say. "The peculiarity of writing in this way is that the lines are necessarily somewhat curved. In producing such writing under a table the operator would by twitchings or shudderings take off attention for a second, and that would suffice to turn the slate over. Another short message would then be written on the under side, and on the slate being produced there would be the appearance of writing on the side which had apparently been next the table. Having two messages written on a slate is of course convenient, for the performer would read the upper one and rubbing it out would say. ' Now we will try again.' Then he would place the other side of the slate against the table and say to his visitor, ' You hold the corner.' Of course the point of the trick is that he turns the slate over beneath the table and then after it has been held close against the table, the writing appears again on the upper surface of the slate. It is easy for a clever conjuror to change the side of a slate in this way." Mr. Maskelyne then demonstrated in court how even with a locked slate writing can be made to appear. The medium would first take the opportunity to write a message on the slate, and then hastily passing a damp sponge over it and rubbing it dry, it would seem to be perfectly clear. The slate would be locked, but in the course of a few minutes the writing would distinctly reappear. This is an easy trick performed with a special pencil, yet by this thousands have been deluded into the belief that they held converse with the dead. Mr. Maskelyne's exposure was most complete. The evidence of some of the other witnesses was most amusing, one gentleman having received affectionate messages from a presumed deceased friend who never existed he having given the "medium" a fictitious name.

On the 29th October Mr. Flowers gave judgment, and said that recollecting the grave results involved, he felt it incumbent upon him to sentence the defendant to three months imprisonment with hard labour. Notice of appeal to the Middlesex Sessions was given, and Slade was released on bail. In January following the appeal was heard. Dr. Slade was represented by three of the ablest counsel at the English bar, and on a legal point the conviction was quashed. But the exposure had been so thorough, that Slade took an early opportunity of flitting to the continent. All these things can be read in the files of the London journals for the dates given I have quoted the reports verbatim.

Slade next turned up in Russia, where, since the days of Home, spiritualism has been fashionable. Then in the end of the year 1877 he appeared in Berlin. In foreign countries as the medium is unacquainted with any language but his own, the spirits could not send written messages, consequently we find Slade's seances chiefly made up of "manifestations" of hanky-panky with rings and chairs. These took place in a dark room and from the published accounts, there was nothing that an expert conjuror could not do. The whole imposture has been fully exposed in the last volume of that highly interesting work, "Wissenschaftliche-Abhandlungen" by Frederich Zollner, published in Leipsic last year. On several occasions, however, the slate trick was performed. The answers were always in English of the stereotyped kind, such as. "we will try," "we cannot tell." "I will answer." The work mentioned contains two lithographs of slates with spirit writing. The first in a back hand runs, "Man's doubts can't change a fact a fact will change his doubts." Spirits do not punctuate, and the second example shows that they are equally reckless of grammar, a circumstance noticed at the seances of the medium in Sydney. This is in a scratchy uneducated handwriting "We feel to bless all those that * * * * * to investigate a subject to unpopular as the subject of spiritualism is at the present but it will not always be so unpopular it will take its place among the * * * of all classes and kinds." The last omitted word is supposed to be "professions." Shortly after this Slade received an intimation from the police that his absence was necessary, and he left seeking fresh fields and new dupes in Australia.

Slade has found many believers here having reduced his charge to ten shillings. The most intelligent of us are often made the fools of our senses, but then we recognize when we are deluded. But the world is still full of dupes, who are everywhere waiting for impostors to defraud them. These are generally of a weak affectionate disposition, often sceptics in religion, or belonging to those branches of the Protestant Church where no great belief is required to enable them to pass through life as fair everyday Christians. The Catholic faith furnishes few spiritualists. The Dupes if they belonged to the old church would give strict adherence to all its rites and be the most ardent supporters of its most extreme doctrines. These are those who must renounce possession of their wills and intelligence—either to an Absolute Church, a woman or a medium. Many may call themselves sceptics but in truth they are miserable in that condition and yearn for something to believe in. They may know or care nothing at all about spiritualism, but attracted to a seance, at first by mere curiosity, a shrewd impostor at once detects his victims. Surprised at first, these will end in a short time in believing not only what the medium tells them but a great deal more. Dr. Knaggs' paper gives the psychological explanation of this.

And now I have a very painful duty to perform in drawing attention to the long advertisement in the Argus of February 18th, inserted by

Mr. Cyril Haviland. This gentleman is a friend of mine, I esteem him highly, and I respect the memory of the lady whose name has so unfortunately been thus thrust before the public I would gladly pass over this in silence, but Mr. Haviland has thrown down the gauntlet to unbelievers in such a defiant style, as the champion of Slade, that it is impossible to do so. I am afraid that anything that appears in this pamphlet will not change his views, but at least it may prevent others from being deceived. Mr. Haviland I am sure believes every word he has written. I again refer to Dr. Knaggs' paper on this point. Let us first see under what conditions this advertisement is framed. For more than a fortnight Mr. Haviland had been under the moral sway of Slade. The medium had passed several nights in his house, and they had travelled to Melbourne together, Mr. Haviland having no earthly business whatever there, but anxious for as long as possible to receive those messages from his wife's spirit, which Slade professed to furnish him with. The advertisement shows the influence under which Mr. Haviland labours. He believes that Slade said this, and did that at their first interview, when as I think all this was brought out afterwards, when the impostor had been often received into the family circle and would pick up words and phrases and nowledge of past events which he would readily utilise. The fraud is too obvious. The hand is that of Haviland, but the voice is Slade's.

I am not going to analyse or attempt seriatim to account for the manifestations described in this advertisement. I refer to the papers of Dr. Knaggs and Mr. Wilton as to Slade's doings here. *Ex uno disce omnes.* If he is detected in one fraudulent trick, I believe all his manifestations are of the same kind. The evidence at the trial in London shows completely how the slate business is managed, and I have tested this myself. Chevalier Thorn, a member of that very clever company, "The Royal Illusionists" now performing here, has privately gone through the evidence of Slade's trial with me and has demonstrated how easy it is for the slate to be manipulated in the manner described. In fact I believe the *seance* with him was much more interesting than one with Slade. Certainly "The Illusionists" every night perform tricks which eclipse anything that Slade or any other medium has attempted. I am much indebted to Chevalier Thorn for his practical explanations showing how a clever conjuror can outdo a medium. He publishes a challenge to Slade which I hope, but hardly think, will be accepted.

But I wish to point out two things to the readers of Mr. Haviland's advertisement. He promises future contributions to the *Banner of Light*, a paper which "has the cause at heart." Now this journal is the same foolish or fraudulent one which when the Davenport Brothers were in Melbourne, and I exposed them, claimed those known and played-out impostors as spiritualists. I have no doubt it will father anything Mr. Haviland says about Slade. But there is one thing in the advertisement which I can contradict. Mr. Haviland states that Slade " whether in Russia, China, Fiji, or any other foreign country" furnishes communications from the spirits in the language of the people to whom they are addressed. Mr. Haviland makes a solemn declaration of the truth of his assertion, and he shows how deeply he is in the clutches of this imposter, when he writes of his own knowledge what Slade must have told him Now the German work before quoted, which gives an impartial account of Slade's doings in Germany, and lithographs of the "spirit writing" and "spirit footmarks" gives all the answers procured from the spirits. They were in English, and bad English at that. And the other day when a friend of mine visited Slade (merely out of curiosity you may be sure), and was asked to write a question to a deceased friend she did so in French. The answer came back from the spirit of her husband *in English*, a language he did not understand! This proves the falsity of the statement which Mr. Haviland is called upon to swear to.

People who wish to be further enlightened as to the fraudulent practices of professional mediums, are referred to Barnum's "Humbugs of the World," and Maskelyne's "Modern Spiritualism." If in this paper I use strong words it is because I feel strongly, a friend of mine having been duped and the holiest feelings of his nature preyed upon by a scoundrel who I trust will yet meet his just reward. To many who will tell me of strange "manifestations" they have seen, of the mysterious sounds and sights they could not account for, of the vagaries of the planchette, &c., I will reply in the words of Hotspur to the spiritualist Glendower. When the latter boasted of his influence over the power of evil, the plain straightforward courageous Englishman claimed to have a more potent spell:—

" And I can teach thee, coz, to shame the devil
  By telling truth !
  If thou have power to raise him bring him hither
  And I'll be sworn I've power to shame him hence."

"THE VAGABOND."

DR. SLADE AND THE SPIRITS.

———o———

(*Reprinted from the* S. M. HERALD, *after revision.*)

IT was with much pleasure that I received a brief communication from my friend Mr. F., inviting me to Sydney on purpose to visit Dr Slade, with the view of personally investigating the so-called spiritual manifestations produced under his influence My friend Mr. F. prides himself upon his liberality of opinion, and in several arguments with me upon the subject, he has maintained that no judgement should be formed upon the subject of Spiritualism without patient, diligent, and exhaustive inquiry. He has for several years been pursuing the matter with that spirit, but up to the present has come to no very decided opinion beyond the conclusion that there is some very mysterious influence at work, which to him is inexplicable. My reputation as an amateur conjuror, and perhaps the very flattering opinion that he had formed of my perceptive faculties, combined with a latent suspicion that Dr. Slade's spiritualism consisted of a very clever illusionist performance, combined to make him select me to assist him in coming to a determination regarding the phenomena as exhibited at Dr. Slade's seances.

In accepting the invitation, I stipulated that my friend, Mr. Matthew Dawson, also an amateur prestidigitarian, should assist us by being present. It was arranged that our seance should take place at half-past 3 in the afternoon of February 7; but hearing that I could possibly have an extra one in the morning, I took advantage of the chance, and, accompanied by a lady friend, I waited upon the doctor at half-past 9 o'clock on Friday morning, and we were courteously afforded an interview. My object in going in the morning was to have a general survey of the method of procedure; this would enable me to plan for the afternoon any feasable means for the detection of jugglery or fraud, should I have reason to suspect such. I may now state that my sole object was an investigation into the truth,—and I went with an unbiassed and impartial mind—determined to give Dr. Slade every courtesy and fair play. In this paper I shall avoid any personalities or expression of opinion with regard to the subject of Spiritualism I merely record facts as observed by myself, and I do so conscientiously and for the public good.

I explained to Dr. Slade that I had come from the country expressly to visit him; though I had arranged for a seance that afternoon I was so anxious to investigate the subject that I hoped he would permit me to see his manifestations at once. He, without hesitation, complied, and ushered us into his room arranged for that purpose. The room was a well-lighted room, carpeted. The furniture consisted of a plain deal table, a few chairs, a small round table, and in the far corner of the room a side table containing a few slates, slate pencils, and other miscellaneous articles of no general import to this paper. At his request I examined the deal table in the centre of the room. I cannot better describe it than an ordinary pine dressing table, without drawers, having its width extended by the addition to each side of a fixed flap, about a foot wide. The framework, each corner of which was supported by the legs, was of small size, so that the top of the table extended about eighteen inches beyond the frame on every side. I estimated that the top of the table was about four feet square. I carefully examined the table, turned it completely over, and looked into every joint. I was convinced that it was bona-fide, and no mechanism whatever existed in it. Upon replacing it, I purposely altered its position on the floor, so as to place its legs out of reach of any electro-magnets, should such be concealed beneath the carpeting—illusionists, amateur or professional will know the import-ance of this proceeding. I carefully examined the carpet for holes through which concealed rods or levers might project to raise tables or chairs. This examination having been satisfactorily concluded, we were seated in such places as requested by Dr. Slade. The light, I think, entered the room on the west side; Dr. Slade took his position at the north side of the table. I was seated on the west side, with my back to the window, my lady friend at the south side facing the doctor. The east side of the table was vacant. On sitting down the doctor specially drew our attention to the way he sat—sideways—he facing the window, and his feet clear of the table. He asked us if we had ever been present at anything of the kind before. He then requested us to place our hands in the usual manner near the centre of the table. We were in this position without any result for about one minute, when he said, " The influence is very strong, I feel great power, you " turning to me " are very mediumistic, we shall soon get some knocks, they will come about there," pointing to the centre of the table. We then heard some knocks in the spot indicated and near to Dr. Slade's side. He informed us they were quite different to ordinary knocks, being in the wood. He then asked the spirits if they would write? three knocks responded, which he informed us was an affirmative. He then, from the side table, produced an ordinary school slate, which I examined. He carefully cleaned it with a sponge, rested a piece of pencil about the size of an oat seed upon it, and held it partly under the table. He said that the influence was so strong that he could not hold it steady. His body, arms, and hand twitched and tremored in a convulsive manner. All this time one of his hands and both of my and my friend's hands were touching in nearly the centre of the table—for fully two minutes this oscillation of the slate continued, sometimes under the table completely out of view, and sometimes over the table. He then requested us to listen, and a distinct scratching sound was heard, as though some writing was being transcribed by a pencil upon the slate. This having ceased, he endeavoured to withdraw it from the table.

but said it stuck to the table, and he had to use much apparent force in drawing it from under the ledge of the table. He then exhibited to us the upper surface of the slate and a piece of pencil was found resting upon it with the following message written lengthways across the slate in a bold distinct hand :— "The more man investigates, the more he will know the laws of the spirits ; one day's investigation will not do much good, investigate at your own homes." Having expressed our astonishment at this remarkable manifestation, Dr. Slade said he would ask the spirits if they would raise the table, and presently the slate was produced, having written upon it—" We will try." He then grasped the leg of the table nearest him, between his knees, buried the ledge of it into his abdomen, requested me to rest my foot upon his toes. He requested us to keep raising our hands upwards. We did so several times, when suddenly the table bodily rose to a height of about 5 inches, remained poised there for twenty seconds, and then descended to the floor with a crash. I must note that during this and the following experiments the doctor's legs were not sideways—away from under the table as he always professed them to be, but he changed his position and placed them directly under the table. He now said he would try and cause a small table to be lifted. This he placed on the floor against the unoccupied side of the square table, exactly facing me, resting his left hand lightly upon it ; in a few seconds it oscillated, and tilted towards my lady friend, which, Dr. Slade informed her, signified that she possessed mediumistic powers. After a few more tiltings the table eventually rose up from the ground to a height of about eight inches. My lady friend here made an effort to look under the table, which caused Dr. Slade suddenly, as if in great pain, to remove his hand from the risen table, when it fell heavily to the ground. I then asked for a special experiment. I told him that I had heard of a handkerchief being placed on a lady's lap and being whisked by some invisible influence into a corner, when it was found to be tied into intricate knots. He gave me the remarkable reply that he never asked the invisibles to do anything for a successful seance, it must be left to their own will to make whatever manifestations they themselves elected. My lady friend incautiously suggested that in the last experiment the small table was touched by his feet, but he asserted that such was impossible, as he sat in such a position that he could not possibly reach it. He now declared that all power had left him, and after making another careful examination of the table, we gave our honorarium, and withdrew.

This seance was very satisfactory to me, and I congratulated myself on having so good a preliminary view of the subject I hoped more fully to investigate that afternoon. In half-an-hour my friend Dawson and I were closely closeted, and during the day had matured our plans.

Punctually at half-past 3 o'clock we presented ourselves according to appointment at Carlton House, Mr. Dawson, Mr. F., Mr. P., and myself. Dr. Slade being engaged, we went into the waiting-room ; in a few moments he came out. I asked him if four persons were too many. He at once recognised me and appeared disinclined towards my being admitted. He said that three with himself would attain better results, that I had better remain out, but Mr. F. at once retired in my favour. We were ushered into his room and the table was carefully examined by Messrs. Dawson and P.

We were arranged by the doctor in a manner just suited to our plans. Mr. Dawson occupied the seat I had used in the morning to Dr. Slade's right. I sat opposite to Dr. Slade, and Mr. P. at the vacant side. This time it will be seen the four sides of the table were occupied Dr. Slade as usual sitting sideways, having his feet clear of the table, and impressing us with that fact.

The manifestations slightly varied from those that I had seen in the morning, thus, while we were hearing knocks elicited in reply to questions by Dr. Slade, Mr. Dawson's chair was suddenly dragged in the direction of Dr. Slade. The doctor declared that he then saw a phosphorescent light upon Dr. Dawson's coat ; we couldn't see the phenomenon, but while trying to do so the chair was again dragged in a similar manner, and while our attention was being thereby attracted towards it, Mr. P's chair, to his consternation, suddenly took a lurch, also in the direction of Dr. Slade. General notice was now directed towards me, and my chair was requested to move but without avail. Next followed the slate writing upon the plain slate, which was done as in the morning. I next produced a log slate which I had brought with me. This was carefully cleaned and a piece of pencil put inside. This slate was held closed in Dr. Slade's hand, and the spirits requested to write upon it. The doctor expected some difficulty to be experienced, in consequence, as he told us, of the slate having a varnished wooden external cover. He requested me and Mr. Dawson to hold the school slate and pencil under the corner of the table between us, and specially directed our attention to listen if any writing took place upon it. While intently doing so, the slate which we held, was twice rapidly pushed outwards in a direction from Dr. Slade by some invisible force. He then drew the log slate from under the table, and having opened it to show us there was nothing written upon the bottom leaf of it, he placed it upon the corner of the table, under his right elbow. He told us to listen, when we heard a scratching sound apparently within the slate, which he at once opened, and the following sentence was found imperfectly written within it :—
" Many a— p—sent but emit—nor emat it nst —ook w inform."
Probably the intention was to say : " Many are present, but must not communicate it—must look for information." This was in reply to a query from Dr. Slade., asking if many spirits were present, and would communicate. The seance concluded with the experiment of causing the table to rise bodily from the floor, which was done in a manner exactly similar to that described as having taken place in the morning. Dr. Slade then declared himself exhausted and unable to proceed any further.

I have so far minutely, and with an accuracy almost to tediousness, described the two seances of Dr. Slade at which I was present. Since boyhood I have been an ardent admirer of conjuring and juggling tricks, and by dint of earnest and continued practice have attained myself an amount of skill in the art rather unusual for an amateur. I mention this as I consider it an eminent qualification for an inquirer into a subject of this nature that he should have some familiarity with the usual procedures necessary for carrying out an exhibition in which deception of the senses forms a conspicuous feature. I was thus enabled to carefully note byplay, and apparently trivial occurrences which played an important part in Dr. Slade's entertainment. I shall, therefore, first point out what circumstances there are in Dr. Slade's performance which favour deception. The very simplicity of the apparatus forms a most conspicuous feature, and makes his manifestations appear the most wonderful and supernatural. Amongst the ancients, and even now with savages and the uneducated, whatever they could not or cannot rationally explain they attributed to the devil. In our days, and amongst many educated people, similar circumstances under similar conditions are attributed to spirits.

At the beginning of each seance the doctor draws special attention to the fact that he always sits sideways, with his feet clear of the table; but it is a strange fact—and to which public attention has never yet been directed—that when the operator and his sitters are seated at the table, with their hands together near its centre, the flap of the table shuts the doctor's legs from out the sitter's vision. Each phenomenon is introduced in an unexpected manner. Dr. Slade tells his sitters that everything must be taken as it comes. Another special feature is the vacillating ways and the uncertainty of the spirits manifesting at all. The slightest exhibition of curiosity on the part of the sitters, or any attempt to take a furtive peep under the table appears mortally to offend the immortals — their manifestations at once cease. The removal of the hands from near the centre of the table, which should be done in order to peep under the table, at once breaks the circle. A psychological feature in the case also is what is claimed by all spiritualists, I believe, namely — the greater the faith there is in spiritualism on the part of the sitter the more remarkable will be the manifestations. In other words, an individual having such faith in Dr. Slade to take as gospel all that he states, will see more wonderful and barefaced things done by him than an inquisitive unbeliever, the deterrent influence of whose presence with sharp scrutinising eyes is at all times most formidable.

Thus had I the benefit of two seances with Dr. Slade, which I attended expressly with the view of examining into the subject of spiritism as demonstrated by him, and having already anticipated the advice of his spirits, written so mysteriously on the slate—"The more man investigates, the more he will know of the laws of the spirits. One day's investigation will not do you much good; investigate at your own homes." I have spent many days upon the subject. I have experimented and investigated at my own home. The result of my study at home as well as my experiences at his seances has been to convince me that Dr. Slade is an exceedingly clever man, but he has nothing whatever to do with spirits. He is no conjuror or illusionist in the ordinary acceptation of the terms. His is quite a new line, one stamped by originality and novelty, and carried out with an energy and dash worthy of admiration, were they only employed in a better cause.

The performance exhibited by Dr. Slade requires all the mental, manual, and mechanical abilities of a first-class prestidigitarian; and in addition, the suppleness of limb and elasticity of joint that can only be acquired by the long continued practice and privations that make a first-class contortionist. With these qualities he has in combination a strong will, a penetrating mind, and a thorough knowledge of human nature in all its phases; he is also an astute physiognomist. For Dr. Slade's performances in this sense I have the greatest respect. I honestly confess that I paid with pleasure the unasked honorarium of half a sovereign at the termination of each sitting. I considered I had value for my money in the lessons I had learnt at his exceedingly clever performances.

The few appliances he has at hand to carry on his deceptions, and the simplicity of the *modus operandi*, while it makes them marvellous to the believing beholders—to unbelievers it remains an extraordinary fact, how he can so long continue to dupe thousands, and notwithstanding so many exposures, to still retain the confidence of the multitude.

The explanation that I am now about to give of the means that he adopts in producing his manifestations will surprise many, and no doubt may cause controversy. I, however, supply as a test the means which I used myself whereby many persons may judge for themselves of the truthfulness of my observation as well as my interpretation of Dr. Slade's spiritual manifestations. The means I adopted and which I now suggest for discovering the deception is to obtain a plain mirror of silvered glass, say two and a half inches wide and five inches long. " Investigate at your homes," and after a few experiments you will soon discover how to place this mirror between your legs at such an angle that when you look down upon it you can, while sitting at the table, reflect the doctor's legs and the underpart of his table. Of course, should the person who proposes to adopt this plan innocently explain his intention to the doctor, the probability will be that he will give his smiling assent, and say that nothing affords him greater pleasure than to give every opportunity for the fullest investigation. Unfortunately the spirits will think differently. There will be no manifestation whatever while the mirror remains *in situ* beneath the table. Spirits easily take offence and don't like to submit to the indignity of being tested. A knowing person, however, with some sleight of hand, will be able to keep his own counsel and use the mirror to his own edification, without either the doctor or the spirits being any the wiser.

The first thing to strike the observer will be the remarkable facility the operator has of moving his legs independently of imparting any motion whatever to his body. Sitting sideways towards the table with his legs apparently in front of him, he is capable of shooting out either leg in any direction, reminding one of the movements of the knee, and writhed his shoulder like one suffering from rheumatic pains in that joint. X. (who had had many previous interviews) here exclaimed that he should like to try "the experiment with the compass;" and the slate business, whatever it was to be, was stopped while the doctor produced an ordinary little brass pocket compass with what appeared to be the usual spring movement to set the needle out of gear when not in use, but which of course, it will be perceived, might have been connected with other concealed mechanism within, required to produce the effects that subsequently occurred. The doctor adjusted the spring so as to set the needle free and placed the compass on the table when X. drew it towards himself. The doctor said he would ask the spirits if they would cause the needle to oscillate, and then, after some tremor of his hand and furtive glances at the slate, still down in the direction of his knee, clapped it up flat to the table underneath, placing his thumb on the upper side, and his fingers below out of sight. In this position I was enabled to see his forefinger for about half an inch below the knuckle, and X. particularly pointed this out to me with the remark that it was impossible anybody could write anything with his hand so fixed. I watched what I could see of the forefinger closely, expecting to observe some muscular movement communicated by the action of the other fingers but none occurred. This however amounts to nothing, for in subsequent experiments, which anyone may verify for himself, I found that a slate may be retained in the position described by the thumb and forefinger, and the other fingers can be moved to and fro underneath without creating the slightest muscular disturbance in the portions of the hand that remain in view. In this case, I think, it was perfectly unnecessary for the doctor to resort to any extraordinary manipulation to produce the writing which in a minute or so was shown to us, for what with "patter" and the interruption caused by the arrangement of the compass, there was time enough to scribble anything on the slate without risk of observation. The doctor held the slate up flat to the underside of the table, and a sound, as of some one writing on it with a pencil, became distinctly audible, lasting but for a second or so, and ending with three rapid taps. The slate was then brought to view, and there appeared on it the words—"We will try." Nothing, however, happened to the compass till Dr. Slade stretched his hand over towards it, and made a quick circular movement above it, backwards and forwards, when the needle commenced to move violently, just as it might if the doctor had a small piece of steel concealed beneath his finger nails. In all fairness, however, I must add, I took particular notice of his finger nails, and observed that they were so closely pared down as to forbid the supposition that he could fix anything as large as a grain of wheat beneath them. But then, again, a very trifling thing will disturb a compass—such, for instance, as a strong magnet, grasped by the operator's toes, and deftly applied to the underside of the table. The doctor told X. to try if he could cause the compass to move, adding, that as he had some mediumistic powers, he might be successful. X. tried his hand, but the movement imparted to the needle by the doctor had not subsided, and I do not think it was prolonged in the slightest degree by any effort that X. made, though he and the doctor thought differently. The compass, however, was very obedient to the doctor, and moved whenever he stretched his hand (and, by the way, it was his *left hand*) over to it. With his right hand he had, in the meantime, cleaned the slate (having had ample time and opportunity to do anything else with it, while our attention was attracted to the compass), and had taken it again beneath the table. At this moment X. gave a start, and Doctor Slade almost instantaneously gave another. "Wul, wul!" exclaimed the latter, with a surprised look, "what was that ? Did you feel anything ?" "Yes," said X, "I felt my leg pushed !" "And I," said the doctor, " nearly had the slate pulled out of my hand." Up to this point nothing had occurred to me. I was sitting with my left leg (that nearest to Doctor Slade) doubled under my chair, while my right leg was thrust under the table, somewhat in a slanting direction towards X., and away from the doctor. Of a sudden, X. said : "There, I have been touched again !" and then I distinctly felt two very light, but distinct, pressures rapidly given, as if by a hand on my right leg, just above the knee. I, however, said nothing, and remained stolid and silent. Doctor Slade then declared that he could see a small light hovering over the compass, but as I could see nothing of the kind, I made no remark ; but the reader will notice that all these observations, though seeming to arise naturally, served to prolong the interval between the slate "manipulations," and gave ample time to the "spirits" to prepare something extraordinary, for all the while the slate was kept below the line of our sight, and I frequently observed the doctor casting stealthy glances down in its direction. At length, after shaking the slate to and fro, as if trying to get the pencil in the centre, he fixed it again beneath the table-top in the same manner as described before, and exclaimed : " Intelligences ! will you favour us with a long message ?" Thereupon there was a scratching as of some one writing, which lasted for quite two minutes ; and, while this was going on, I felt two more rapid pressures on the right leg, but gave no outward sign. The result was just what I expected. Still holding the slate against the table, the scratching sound going on without intermission, Dr. Slade threw himself slowly back in his chair, as if changing his position, merely to give relief to the muscles of his back ; but watching him I saw his eyes glance rapidly beneath the table, in the direction of my leg, as if to make sure of its exact position. He then leaned forward again, and, in a second or so, I was favoured with two more touches, but, as before, took not the slightest notice of them, and *they were not again repeated*. It wanted no spirit to produce such an absurd manifestation as this. An extension of Dr. Slade's leg beneath the table, and a prehensile movement of his foot were the causes to which I attributed the effect directly I felt the first touches. By remaining silent, I thought, I should puzzle him, and it fell out as I expected. Having administered two doses of "spirit" touches, without producing in me any visible sign of astonishment, it occurred to him, I fancy, that he had been giving my friend X. the experiences

be intended for me, and hence the necessity for his leaning back and
gauging the exact position of my leg. Making sure then that he touched
me the next time, and finding that I preserved silence, he became
aware that I was on the watch, and stopped all further "manifestations" of that kind. The scratching beneath the table having ceased,
the slate was produced, and the whole side of it was covered with
writing, in a clear, bold, regular hand, entirely different to the clumsy
characters in which the message—"we will try,"—had been written.
This difference, I suppose, will be hailed as proof by some people of
the genuineness of the "manifestation;" but as after the receipt
of the first message X. had told the doctor that many people
alleged the writing to be always the same, I was not at all
surprised to find the next communication in another hand.   There
were about twenty lines now on the slate, which the doctor read
out to us, and almost immediately afterwards commenced to rub out.
The precise wording of the message I cannot remember; but its pur-
purport was to the effect that the "angels" were pleased to find us
devoting ourselves to such an investigation as we were engaged in—
that we were to search diligently and patiently, and in time great
truths would be revealed to us, and it ended with the admonition that
the "intelligences" were indisposed to hold any communication with
those who were impressed with unbelief. X. said the latter remark
must be intended to apply to me. I replied, "possibly so, but that
any unbelief I might feel did not take an offensive form."   And now
a circumstance occurred which is worthy of note.   The doctor had
risen from his chair during X's remark, and having placed one of his
feet upon it commenced to rub and move the joints like one who
suffered from twinges of cramp. He had had plenty of time to use
his fingers; but had he been writing with his toes? Or had the prehensile movement necessary to produce "spirit" touches given him
the cramp? Without saying anything, however, he resumed his seat,
and taking the slate in his right hand, leaned over in my direction and
placed it underneath the table in front of my body, leaving about an
inch or so exposed to view immediately beneath my eyes.   On the
instant, before I could look up, the vacant chair opposite to me was
flung violently backwards against the wall.   X. gave a start of surprise, and Dr. Slade threw himself back in the chair, with a rolling
motion, as if recovering his balance and exclaimed in tones of amused
astonishment : " Wal, wal! Really, I declare now! Ain't it cur'ous ?"
I said nothing, though I am convinced the disturbance of the chair
was due to a vigorous kick administered by the doctor himself, while
our attention was directed to his manoeuvring with the slate.

X. now suggested that I should ask some questions of the spirits,
and the slate was handed to me by Dr. Slade and I wrote this : "Can
you tell me how ——— met with his death?" The slate was taken
from me by Dr. Slade with that side of it on which my question was
written turned downwards. He placed a small piece of pencil on the
blank surface, and went through the usual nervous performance,
carrying the slate far below the level of the table, and again I saw
his eyes glance stealthily down in its direction, and I felt quite certain

limbs of a cuttle-fish. His foot and flexible toes in his thin, very thin,
kid slippers, possess the mobility of a human hand in a glove. It is by
means of the foot that he makes the taps underneath the table—that
he grasps the sitters' chairs and drags them towards him, or pushes
them from him. In the use of his feet and toes his dexterity is marvellous. The slate writing is the most clever part of his performance.
Like many illusionists he has more than one string to his bow, and
does not always do the same feat in the same way. In writing long
communications which fill up several lines the whole length of
the slate, the writing is done by the pencil being grasped by
the toes, or else fixed in the slipper of the left foot. Short communications such as "Yes," "No," "I will try," usually found to be written
transversely across the slate, and not very straightly, are done by a
pencil between the fingers of the hand holding the slate. In no case
does the minute piece of pencil, which is placed upon the slate
contribute towards the writing. A sharp observer may also find that
it is not the same piece of pencil which is put on the slate previous to
the inscribing that is found thereon subsequently. The following is
one of the methods of procedure for writing upon a common school
slate :—The slate is cleaned most carefully—this is very important,
the object being that both sides of the slate shall be so similar that
one side cannot be identified from the other—a very small piece of
pencil is rested upon the slate, which is partly out of sight beneath
the table, and now begins what conjurors call "business" and
"patter." The operator's arms twitch—the hands of sitters are
arranged and rearranged so as to ensure good results—the slate is
floated about, still being held by the operator's hand, is made to rest
upon the sitter's shoulder, and occasionally disappears under the table.
It is during this business that the operator noiselessly with either his
foot or fingers writes upon the under surface of the slate. The
rapidity or dexterity with which this is done under the table is
admirable. The upper unwritten surface of the slate and piece of
pencil are once more exhibited ; the slate then placed under the table,
while for an instant out of sight, is dexterously turned over ; its edges
are now ostentatiously exhibited under the ledge of the table. The
sitters are requested to listen. A scratching sound is heard. On its
ceasing the slate is drawn with apparent force from under the table.
To the surprise of all the surface of the slate, seen clean, as they
thought, a moment before, is found to have a lengthy communication
upon it. The piece of pencil is also found to have a face worn upon it
by the action of the writing, a very skilful accessory to the illusion
easily explained.

The writing on the log slate is done in a similar manner, its very
construction aiding the illusion. Holding it by the corner at which it
opens, that is at edge away from the hinges, the usual business and
patter is gone through. At my second seance, it will be remembered,
that Mr. Dawson and I were requested to manipulate with the school
slate while the doctor was trying to obtain writing in the log slate.
Seizing his opportunity while the slate is out of sight, the flap is
dropped and a communication is noiselessly written upon the under

19

surface of the upper flap—the minute piece of pencil replaced—the slate is now produced, partly but cautiously opened, and it is shown that no writing is upon the slate surface of the lower flap—the written surface of the upper flap being kept out of view in consequence of the position in which it is being held—brief business and patter are now gone through, the position of slate changed—a scratching is heard—the slate opened and an apparent miracle performed—writing is found inside the slate, which a moment before was exhibited without writing, and since then had not been out of view.

The great feature giving effect to this illusion is that the writing is done noiselessly, while the sitter's attention is otherwise occupied. I have reason to think also that the writing is done by a softer slate pencil than that ostensibly exhibited as being used by the spirits—the use of a soft pencil would ensure the writing to be noiseless. I quietly pocketed the piece of pencil said to have written upon my own log slate—the facet upon it did not correspond with the broad soft outlines of the spirit writing which I still retain upon my slate.

I need not occupy much more time with Dr. Slade's very clever performances. The raising of the table bodily from the floor—in order to do which he grasped one leg of the table between his legs and knees, and buried the edge of the table top into his abdomen, was merely a feat of muscular power no doubt acquired by continual practice. The many extraordinary feats that we hear of having been done by him before firm believers in spiritualism, upon analytical inquiry, and making due allowance for human gullibility and his great penetration into human character, will be found to resolve themselves into natural phenomena, easily explained, but greatly magnified.

In conclusion, I may state that had Dr Slade come here as a conjurer, nothing would have induced me to expose his very clever manipulation. As he in his performances contributes towards the dissemination of a new religion, founded on what I hope in another paper to prove to be a highly infectious mental disease, I deem it my public duty to publish this result of my inquiry into the subject.

SAMUEL T. KNAGGS, M.D., F.R.C.S., &c.

Newcastle, New South Wales.

NOTE.—Mr. Matthew J. Dawson accompanied Dr. Knaggs in his visit to Slade, and corroborates all the above statements, and particularly as to the manner in which the table was lifted. He also states :—" I can affirm that on the second occasion of my chair being moved, I distinctly saw Dr. Slade's foot do it. Just previous to this manœuvre he tried to draw our attention to a phosphorescent light, which he said was upon my left shoulder, though I moved my head as though to do so instead of looking at the shoulder, I glanced downwards and detected him in the act."

ANOTHER SEANCE WITH DR. SLADE.

———o———

In confirmation of the account given by Dr. Knaggs, of the two *séances* which he had with Dr. Slade and "the spirits," I wish to give a narrative of the occurrences that fell within my own experience at a similar exhibition of the so-called medium's powers.

Like Dr. Knaggs, I have over been fond of conjuring feats, and have attained, by practice, some little proficiency in their execution. I am therefore not a novice in the artifices necessary to be employed to secure success in the performance of tricks of illusion, and in witnessing them, am not easily thrown off my guard at those critical moments, when, for the accomplishment of his purpose, it is necessary that the executant should distract the attention, and elude the vigilance of his audience by some cleverly executed feint in an opposite direction. Here, let me say that I know nothing of spiritualism, except what I have read, and that previous to my interview with Dr. Slade, I had only once been present at "a circle" where, however, the "manifestations" were of an exceedingly poor character, and ever since they have been associated in my mind with an easily explained self-deception on the part of those engaged in their production. I have often essayed to evoke the phenomena with the assistance of friends of a practical turn of mind, but have always utterly failed to produce anything whatever. Tables refuse to tilt themselves at my bidding, chairs remain stoically fixed. No knocks come in response to any entreaty addressed to the "spirits," or "intelligences." Pianos won't play without hands, tambourines won't fly round and hit people on the head, no bell will ring, concertinas remain dumb, and I never can get a handkerchief, by any coaxing, to tie itself into knots. Believers in the "spirits," when I tell them these things, condescendingly bestow sweet smiles of pity upon me, shrug their shoulders at my benighted state, and say that I shall never obtain "manifestations,," because I am not a believer. They assure me I must approach the Unseen (with a capital U, please) in an entirely different spirit. I must repose unfaltering belief in them, and solicit their confidence with the simplicity and confiding trust of a child; then, and not till then, shall I be rewarded with their intimacy. I have tried the childlike simplicity business, and offered myself as a votary to the belief of anything; presenting my mind to the spirits free from guile its normal state, as my friends will admit) but all to no purpose, the spirits remain obdurate, and treat me as a Pariah. I approach them humbly, asking for something to believe—anything they like to offer, but they will give me nothing, evidently determined to let me die of the hunger and thirst I have for knowledge. I have sometimes thought that I have not the right sort of furniture for spiritualistic purposes, though it looks like other people's; but I am assured by true believers that the sole cause of failure lies in my want of faith: that my desire to investigate any phenomena that may be presented, gives mortal offence to the spirits, and that in resentment they withhold all "manifestations" from me. However, I have no desire to enter into a controversy with spiritualists, or to question the grounds or genuineness of their belief. All I know is that I can get none of the indications out of chairs and tables that are vouchsafed to other people, and am firmly convinced I never shall. My present business is with Dr. Slade, whose spiritual performances I most unhesitatingly declare to be nothing more than cunningly devised illusions throughout.

In the interview I had with Dr. Slade (which I will describe presently) some two or three things occurred that puzzled me at the time, but which the excellent narrative and explanation given by Dr. Knaggs have rendered perfectly plain now to my comprehension. I, on the other hand, noticed occurrences which, if they did not escape his observation, have not been alluded to by him, and they certainly cleared up all doubt in my mind as to the manner in which certain other effects were produced. So if Dr. Knaggs did not notice them, my allusion to them here will perhaps serve to strengthen his convictions upon the subject.

It was in the beginning of February that Mr. X. (a firm believer in the genuineness of Dr. Slade's mediumistic powers) called upon me at 11 a.m., and invited me to accompany him to Carlton House, Wynyard Square, to have a seance with the doctor, a proposition with which I gladly complied. Arriving at the house we found the doctor to be engaged, and were shown into a waiting-room until he was at liberty to · receive us. In a few minutes a tall well-dressed gentlemanly man entered the room, smiling, with whom my friend shook hands, and announced as Dr. Slade. I was introduced, and the object of our visit being explained, the doctor said he would give us a sitting at once, and we then adjourned to the room which has been so minutely described by Dr. Knaggs, and the surroundings of which I mentally took in directly we entered. My chief interest, however, was centred in observation of Dr. Slade himself. His figure was well proportioned, and showed much muscular power, while his movements exhibited great litheness and activity. His features were handsome and pleasing in their openness of expression, his manner engaging, attractive, and self-possessed, while the tones of his voice were suggestive of much candour and simplicity. He had a slight American accent, and altogether was most prepossessing in deportment and general appearance. In the centre of the room stood the deal table described by Dr Knaggs, which X. tilted up and said I was at perfect liberty to examine. I did so and am convinced there is no mechanism about it. It is about four feet square, and its only peculiarity is that its legs and their connecting framework are placed close enough together to allow the top to project beyond them about 14 or 15 inches. In describing this table Dr. Knaggs speaks of its width being "extended by the addition to each side of a fixed flap," and this, I find, has given to many readers a wrong impression of its construction, nearly everybody associating the word "flap" with something which can be moved at will. Suffice it to say, that the boards of which the table top is made have simply been cut to the length required, and are perfectly immoveable. It presents the peculiarity of a table in the construction of which the maker has by accident fixed on a top intended for a much larger framework, and except that it is exceedingly light, it has nothing remarkable about it but its extreme simplicity of construction, a feature, by the way which Dr. Slade pointed out with the remark that it had been made in Sydney "by an honest Chinaman." Having examined the table, it was placed upright again on the carpeted floor by X. and Dr. Slade evinced no anxiety in its adjustment, clearly attaching no importance whatever to its precise situation.

We were then requested to be seated. There were four chairs in position around the table—one at each side facing each other. My friend was told to take the one at the end facing Dr. Slade, and I was requested to occupy that at the side on the right hand of the doctor, which placed me with my back to the window. It has since occurred to me that by this arrangement I was removed from the observation of any shadows which might have been cast beyond the line of the table by any movements of the medium beneath. As we sat, we occupied three sides of the table, and opposite to me stood the vacant chair, of which more anon. We then placed our hands on the table in the centre in a heap, Dr. Slade's covering ours, when instantly a slight tapping sound commenced, which I could not connect with the table ; but of which no notice was taken by X. or the doctor. The latter, however, directed my attention to the fact that he was sitting with his feet sideways in the direction of the window, and looking down I ascertained that to be the case, observing at the same time that the doctor's feet were encased in those morocco slippers which, having no heels, enable the feet to glide in and out so comfortably without trouble. I also observed that the texture of his socks was as fine as silk—a feature of some importance if his feet are required, at these séances, to produce effects demanding delicacy of touch and dexterity in movement. No other knocks came, and Dr. Slade produced a common deal-framed little slate with some tiny pieces of slate pencil. The latter he threw upon the table while he cleaned the former with a piece of sponge. Here let me say that throughout the interview Dr. Slade kept up a running fire of small talk, uttered in a charmingly natural manner, and which I very soon set down as "patter." Having cleaned the slate to his satisfaction, the doctor placed a thin piece of pencil upon it, about an eighth of an inch long, and keeping his left hand on ours, removed the slate in a horizontal position with his right hand, and placed it, or tried to place it, under the ledge of the table. He was, however, prevented in the accomplishment of this design by a sudden tremulousness which agitated his wrist and hand to such a degree, as to make the slate clatter against the table like a castanet. He said he was "always like this," and lowered his hand with the slate down to about the level of his he turned the slate in his fingers, and so read what I had written. While this movement was being executed some general talk was indulged in, and then the slate was brought up against the under side of the table. An audible scratching again occurred, which terminated with the taps as before, when the slate was brought to view with this answer legibly written upon it : " We do not know how he met with his death." This answer, if disappointing. was certainly candid. Moreover it had the additional merit of getting rid in a decisive manner, of a very awkward question. There are so many ways in which people may die. The " spirits " perhaps objected to particularise the precise disease or manner of death in this instance. Perhaps they objected to being run into such a corner! The slate was again cleaned and placed under the table, more scratching was heard, and this time the message, written on it was alleged to be intended for my friend X., and had reference to something that had occurred at previous seances with the doctor of which I had no knowledge, nor are the public interested in knowing more than that my friend seemed perfectly satisfied with its genuineness.

So far I had seen nothing which in any way puzzled me to explain or account for : or, in other words, that could not have been produced by any clever manipulator, by natural means, without the aid of mechanism of any kind. Now came two "manifestations" which I could not understand, but which, thanks to Dr. Knaggs and his mirror, I comprehend now. X asked Dr. Slade to try if the spirits would take the slate out of his hand, carry it to the other end of the table, and return it him again. He assented. and then turned to me, saying that, in order to show there was no trickery of any kind, he would place his two feet close together and allow me to place my left foot upon them. Accordingly he did so, but in the position in which I sat I could only effectually cover and feel his right foot, and though the toe of my boot projected somewhat over his left it was at an upward angle, and I doubt if it did more than rest gently on the surface of the slipper which covered his left foot. Bending over to my side of the table he then thrust nearly the whole of the slate horizontally beneath it, some two or three inches below the top, and in a second or so it left his hand, and could be heard banging against the framework below in its passage to the other side, where it showed half of its length above the line of the table, flapped i self forcibly against the edge. disappeared, repeated the banging on its way back, and delivered itself into the doctor's hand. This looked mysterious at the time, and I confess puzzled me exceedingly ; but on reading Dr. Knagg's communication to the *Herald* I saw at once the feat could be performed with perfect ease by anyone who had trained his pedal extremities to any moderate degree of muscular flexibility. In my opinion the unseen power that took the slate from Dr. Slade's hand was situated in the toes of Dr. Slade's left foot, which he had withdrawn from its slipper for the purpose and deftly returned to its place on completing the performance, for it, was there when I looked down again. Talking of slippers, by the way, how easy it would be to have a framework in them which would withstand pressure, and leave the wearer at perfect liberty to withdraw both his feet and return them again, without running any great risk of discovery!

The last and crowning manifestation was the raising of the table bodily, from the floor; but this in the first attempt was marred by my want of experience in the means to be adopted to produce the effect. We sat with our hands clustered on the table, and in a second or so, the doctor and X raised their hands up perpendicularly with a tremulous motion, when I felt a weak but distinct motion in the table, as if attempting to rise; but it could not get off the ground on my side, and after an ineffectual struggle for a second or so it dropped again, and Dr. Slade turned suddenly towards me and said "Oh, you must lift up your hands too." I apologized, saying that I was not aware of what was required of me, and asked him to try the experiment again. We all raised our hands simultaneously clear of the table next time, and it followed them with a steady motion straight upwards for a distance perhaps of a foot, and then suddenly dropped. I observed nothing which solved this seeming mystery, and to Dr. Knaggs the credit is due of discovering the artifice employed to secure the "manifestation." The doctor then announced that the spirits would do nothing more, which remark, like the playing of the National Anthem at an ordinary entertainment, was simply a polite way of informing us that the séance was over and thereupon X, and I took our leave.

Now, in conclusion, I wish to reiterate that I have no desire to ridicule those who believe in Spiritualism, or to impugn their veracity in the accounts they give of their experiences. I only speak of things within my own knowledge; and, while pitying my crass ignorance, perhaps Spiritualists will extend their forgiveness to me if I have not that india-rubber quality of faith which prevents my blindly accepting as mysteries, occurrences which if submitted to critical investigation, appear to me to admit of an easy solution as flowing from natural causes. I consider Dr. Slade's "manifestations" to be nothing more than clever conjuring or juggling. In some respects they exceed the feats of ordinary professionals, because they are done in broad daylight, and immediately under the eyes of his audience. But in other respects they show much inferiority. The professional conjuror goes to work in a more straightforward manner, for he generally lets you know what effect he is going to produce beforehand, and challenges you to detect him if you can. But your medium does not, except in rare cases, admit you to any share of his confidence. He deals in surprises, and to secure them, he adopts all sorts of ruses, as for instance, in the kicking over a chair, as described above. Then again he evades inquiry, by laying down the convenient fiction that the spirits will not be dictated to, and that you must accept what manifestations they choose to give and not what you would like to have. Further, that the spirits are so capricious that, while they appear to be very ready to hold communication with the living, they will have nothing to do with unbelievers, or persons anxious to elicit the truth and reality of their proceedings. Give an ordinary conjuror such

conditions as these and he would produce "manifestations" of a far
more astounding character than the silly tricks which form the stock-
in-trade of the so-called spiritual mediums. But, I know of old, it is
of no use arguing with those who accept as genuine the pretended
phenomena evolved under the superintendence of accepted mediums.
They will hold no argument upon the subject, nor will the mediums
submit their feats to any satisfactory test. If any grievance is felt as
to the manner in which Dr. Slade's performances have been criticised,
it will be very easy to give a practical refutation to all that has been
written. Let Dr. Slade submit his manifestations to a committee of
practical men, under conditions that will ensure a crucial test. If he
will not do this, neither he nor his disciples must complain if his
pretended mysteries are denounced as a villainous imposture and
fraud.

THOMAS T. WILTON.

HINDOO JUGGLING AND CHRISTIAN CREDULITY.

I HAVE been asked for a paper descriptive of a few of the "cunning
tricks of hand" and seemingly inexplicable phenomena which as a long
sojourner in the interior of India, that land of mystery, it has been
my privilege ofttimes to witness. Some of these phenomena are to my
mind, far more wonderful than even the most marvellous manifestations claimed by the so-called mediums, yet they are all I believe
capable of an explanation consistent with well known mental or
physical laws, and in no case that I am aware of, is supernatural or
spiritual interposition even suggested much less claimed in their
accomplishment.

The manifestations of mediums differ from ordinary juggling in
this, that they claim direct spiritual interposition. I fully and frankly
admit there may be phenomena which are difficult of explanation to
the ordinary observer. Many of those who have been the most
patient investigators of these phenomena for years are yet unable to
account for them, while rejecting the hypothesis that the spirits of the
dead perform them, while one amiable but rash *gobe mouche* of a
convert, after a few week's experience of Slade's trickery, publishes to
the world his adherence *in toto* to all that Slade says, and boldly
avows that his mushroom religion is "gnawing away the roots
of the old church." Poor fellow! his half-guineas had much
better be expended in buying advice from Dr. Tucker, than in filling
the coffers of the so-called Dr. Slade. The rappings and tappings, the
scratchings, movements of tables and chairs, and writing, &c., are done

they, the mediums, say by the spirits of the dead, who have been summoned from the "unknown land beyond the grave" to revisit these "glimpses of the moon" to, in some undeniable cases at least, gratify a silly curiosity, pander to a morbid craving after excitement, put money into the pockets of proved knaves, or obey the behests and questionings of persons of impure lives, unfeeling hearts, greedy grasping natures, and last though not least limited or imperfect grammar. Detected as quacks, frauds and impostors in one city, they, the mediums, betake them to "fresh fields and pastures new," where they practice their impudent and sacrilegious trade of imposture, and gull and cheat and despoil a fresh set of credulous victims: and such is the gullibility of human nature, that, taken in conjunction with the finer feelings and cherished longings and yearning after renewed intercourse with dear departed friends, which are more or less present in the heart of every affectionate mourner, these unfeeling despi able knaves basely betray the tenderest and holiest aspirations of our natures, desecrate the shrine of purest affection and most ardent love, and degrade and defile the memories of our lost friends by making their so-called spirits, stoop to meannesses and puerilities, which they would have been the first to reprobate with abhorrence when they lived amongst us, loaded with all the imperfections and weaknesses of earth.

We are all so prone to invest what we do not understand, or cannot readily explain, with a supernatural character, that many ill-balanced minds take upon trust the wonderful tales they hear of what mediums can do. They see a few juggling manifestations which deceive their senses, but which are really less wonderful than thousands of the tricks a second rate conjuror can do, and straightway they take all for granted, yield up their whole belief to the delusion and become an easy prey to the spoiler whose trade it is to fatten on credulity, and grow rich on the self deception of the multitude.

There are hundreds of our readers who pooh pooh all this as the language of exaggeration. Convinced in their own minds of the absurdity of the pretensions put forth by these charlatans, the mediums, they think a publication of this kind very supererogatory, in fact calculated to do more harm than good. Are they aware that spiritualism as preached and practised by convicted felons, by meretricious adventurers, by procuresses, by clever plausible scoundrels, has sapped and is sapping the foundations of the religious faith of many, has brought discord and disunion into many a happy home, has impoverished many an impressionable loving credulous nature; has even caused reason to totter on his throne, and is now working incalculable ill to hundreds of families and friends in our very midst.

As a writer in the *Quarterly Review* pertinently says, "To the class of earnest and rigorous inquirers, whom the true philosopher, whatever be his pursuit, welcomes as his most valuable coadjutors, the spiritualists and their allies have ever shown a decided repugnance. 'All or nothing' seems to be the motto of the latter, who act as if a rational explanation of any one of their marvels were a thing to be deprecated. In order to reconcile this discouraging treatment with their professions of readiness to court investigation, they have had recourse to the hypothesis, that just as a damp atmosphere around an electrical machine prevents a high state of electric tension, the presence of even a candid sceptic weakens the mediumistic force, or willingness of the spirits to communicate; and this not merely when he manifests his incredulity by his language, his tones, or his looks, but when he keeps it concealed beneath the semblance of indifference."

Being myself a "candid sceptic" in so far as regards a belief in so called spiritualistic phenomena, I need not of course address myself to believers in spiritualism. If they are not convinced by the expose of Dr. Knaggs, no argument of mine would affect them. "In all ages" says the same reviewer, "the 'possession' of men's minds by 'dominant ideas' has been most complete when these ideas have been *religious* aberrations—the origin of such aberrations has uniformly lain in the preference given to the feelings over the judgment—in the inordinate indulgence of emotional excitement without adequate control on the part of the rational will. Such persons are no more to be argued with than are insane patients. They place themselves beyond the pale of any appeals to their reasoning faculty, and lead others into the same position. They cannot assent to any proposition which they fancy to be in the least inconsistent with their prepossessions; and the evidence of their own feelings is to them the highest attainable truth. It is not to these we have addressed ourselves."

"Ephraim is joined to idols; let him alone." But we would save from this pseudo-religious pestilence, those who are yet unharmed by it, and who may find themselves unexpectedly smitten by its baleful poison.

My descriptions and statements can be substantiated by hundreds of gentlemen who have lived in India, and have seen the same tricks that I have seen. I state on the word of a gentleman that I am not exaggerating or falsifying in any way, and my readers will perhaps therefore dispense with the formula of an affidavit or oath before any magistrate or notary, and where I obtrude my own opinion, they will just take it as they would take that of any ordinary sensible, educated, observant, and thinking person of their acquaintance.

Dr. Slade claims or professes to be able to call up any spirit that may be wanted, and if at Pekin, Hongkong, or Fiji, the spirit will answer in the language in which it is accosted. If he will call up any of my old factory servants, and give or write me an answer to one query, which I will write beforehand and give to a friend, to show there is no wish to deceive on my part, and if the answer be in good *Tirhutya Hindostanee*, I will then begin to doubt my present judgment. If it be objected that I am a sceptic, and the spirits will not come at my call or on my account, let the most bigoted believer in spiritualism ask the question, and if he or she elicit the answer. I will withdraw all present allegations of fraud and imposture, and humbly apologise.

A much-respected friend has gently chid me for wishing to bet on the subject, as he says if the spiritualists are only anxious for an elucidation of the truth, no money stimulus or hope of gain is necesmary. It would only be an insult to a conscientious medium to imagine that he would do for the love of gain, what he would refuse to do from an honest, single-hearted wish to establish right and elicit the truth.

Witchcraft is a firmly settled and popular belief in India. In my lately published book* in Chapter VII., I give a few instances of some rather curious cases I have seen. There are a class of lazy, good-for-nothing, plausible, hypocritical, scoundrelly Brahmins, called Ojahs, who correspond somewhat to our modern professional mediums. These Ojahs are professed witch-finders. They lay claim to great powers, to command occult influences. Some of the things I have seen them do are really wonderful. *Yet they never lay claim to do anything by the agency of spirits.* I doubt not many of them are mesmerists, and mesmerism admits of quite a scientific explanation, as does electro-biology, hypnotism, and other kindred forces. Here is an extract frm my book. At page 66, speaking of witches, I say as follows:—"A blight attacks the melon or cucumber beds; a fierce wind rises during the night and shakes half the mangoes off the trees; the youngest child is attacked with teething convulsions; the plough bullock is accidentally lamed, or the favourite cow refuses to give milk. In every case it is some '*Dyne*,' or witch that has been at work with her damnable spells and charms. I remember a case in which a poor little child had had convulsion The Ojah or witch-finder—in this case a fat, greasy, oleaginous knave, was sent for. Full of importance, and blowing like a 'porpus,' he came and caused the child to be brought to him under a tree near the village. I was passing at the time, and stopped out of curiosity. He spread a tattered cloth in front of him, and muttered some unintelligible gibberish unceasingly, making strange passes with his arms. He put down a number of articles on the cloth—which was villainously tattered and greasy—an unripe plantain, a handful of rice, of parched peas, a thigh bone, two wooden cups, some balls, &c., &c., all of which he kept constantly lifting and moving about, keeping up the passes, and muttering all the time.

The child was a sickly looking, pining sort of creature, rocking about in evident pain, and moaning and fretting just as sick children do. Gradually, its attention got fixed on the strange antics going on. The Ojah kept muttering away, quicker and quicker, constantly shifting the bone and cups and other articles on the cloth. His body was suffused with perspiration, but in about half-an-hour the child had gone off to sleep, and attended by some dozen old women, and the anxious father, was borne in triumph off to the house."

Can any of Dr. Slade's spirits do as much for a sickly suffering child? Another time one of Mr. D's. female servants got bitten by a scorpion. The poor woman was in great agony, with her arm swelled up, when an Ojah was called in. Setting her before him, he began his incantations in the usual manner, but made frequent passes over her body, and over the bitten place. A gentle per-

---

* Sport and Work on the Nepaul Frontier. - Macmillan and Co., 1878.

spiration began to break out on her skin, and in a very short time
the Ojah had thrown her into a deep mesmeric sleep. After
about an hour she awoke perfectly free from pain. In this case
also no doubt the Ojah was a mesmerist.

I had an old *chowkreydar*, or factory watchman, named Seonath
Gopel. He was a very tall, muscular, finely-made man, but totally
blind. Our factory allowed him four rupees a month, merely for the
protection of his name. So long as Seonath got his four rupees the
factory bullocks were safe. He levied a sort of black-mail from the
ryots, or cultivators, all round. If they paid Seonath a little present
every year, their bullocks and cattle were safe from theft. Other
indigo factory managers, from far and near, whenever their bullocks
were stolen, sent the *chowdkrey*, or bullock-keeper, with a present to
Seonath; and *in every case* he would tell them where to find the stolen,
strayed, or lost cattle. *Seonath was a professed medium!* He professed
to get his information from a spirit. He was held in great reverence
by all the natives for leagues around. Many European planters
actually believed in him. The cattle of those who paid him money
were never stolen. Often, if the payments ceased, the cattle mysteriously disappeared. On one occasion, three of my finest plough
bullocks were stolen. My *jemadar*, or head man, said: "Send for
Seonath." I did. I did not ask him to communicate with his spirits,
but I peremptorily told him that, if the bullocks were not back in
three days, I would fine him twenty rupees. *The bullocks were brought
back within the time.* No one could say by whom, but they were
brought back. I could multiply instances. Seonath was revered.
He was a sacred man among the poor deluded natives. They
thoroughly believed in his pretensions. Cattle certainly *were* stolen,
but a visit to Seonath, and a transfer of coin, resulted in a message
from the spirits that the cattle would be found after a certain time at
a certain specified place. *In no instance did the spirits speak falsely.*
Just at that time, and at the very place, the cattle would be forth-
coming. It was mysterious; it was marvellous to the native mind—
inexplicable. What more could a spiritualist wish in the way of
evidence?

I was a "candid sceptic." So was our District Superintendent of
Police. So were some of his astute native detectives. After much
patient investigation, cunningly devised traps, and long weary
waiting, we solved the mystery—we actually captured the spirits.
Seonath had nine sons of his own,—six brothers with families of sons,
and they were all, every man Jack of them, experts in the art and
science of cattle-lifting. It was a family confederacy. Never existed
more practised thieves. Seonath himself planned every theft. A
victim was selected, and on the determined night, his fold would be
visited, relays of the clever thieves hurried the animal by jungly paths
and devious ways, miles and miles away. 'Ere the theft would be
discovered the stolen animal might be, perhaps, beyond the Ganges.
Then, of course, followed the application to Seonath. The spirit
spoke; the bullock or cow was reconveyed to the specified spot, and
each successive restitution was hailed by the credulous natives as

another proof of Seonath's wondrous communication with spiritland. Most of the members of the gang were seized and sent to gaol; Seonath himself, blind as he was, escaped to Nepaul. Possibly, he was warned by the spirits of what was in store for him. With his departure cattle-stealing ceased in that district. Spiritualists are not so numerous there either as formerly.

We hear much of Slade, lifting a chair with a nine-stone female in it bodily from the ground, by merely placing his hand on the back of the chair. The spectator is, of course, in front. Slade is behind the chair, and the drapery of the occupant thereof conceals Slade's legs. What more easy then for him, practised athlete as he is, with the muscles of his legs educated well to do this kind of work, to lift the chair by the bottom bar. Let my reader practice this trick himself, beginning with slight weights. After he has been at it as long as Slade, he will attain equal success. Will Dr. Slade do this, if Dr. Knuggs and myself, or any other "candid sceptic," are standing behind the chair? No. "Sometimes the spirits do it, and sometimes they don't."

I have seen a village juggler do a much more wonderful trick than that. It was at Sonepore fair, in 1872 or '73. It is called the floating trick—suspending a body in the air without any visible support. Dr. Sylvester did the trick here, but experts well know that an iron or steel rod projects from the back of the stage, being hidden by the seemingly floating body. The conjuror passes his sword *apparently* all round in every direction, meeting no resistance on any side. It *does* seem inexplicable. In the case I saw in India it was done in a *shamiana*, that is, under a covered canopy. A young girl was seemingly suspended in mid-air. The green turf was beneath, the canvas walls of the *shamiana* above and on every side. 'Tis true, the English spectators all sat on one side. Yet there were natives all round, and they seemed as astonished as we were. I could not account for it, but the *jadugar*, or juggler, expressly told us, in answer to repeated queries, that it was a trick learned from his father,—a pure deception of the senses. Let spiritualists say it was the spirits if they choose. I believe the juggler himself, although I cannot explain how the thing was done.

The same juggler on the same occasion did a trick which I have often seen done, and have heard explained, but which always seemed to me very wonderful. It is the well known bus et trick. I never saw it better done than by a handsome young juggler from Benares who used to amuse me by his "hanky-panky" one time I was confined to my couch by an attack of rheumatism. The scene of operations was my own verandah. A well built, plastered brick floor. Natives squatting on their hams all around, watching with eager interested looks, every movement of the light, supple, handsome young "Jadugar." His body was bare from the waist upwards, and his long coal black hair was tied behind in a knot. He had none of the ordinary impediments or accessories. He produced a narrow oblong cane-work basket which I was allowed to examine. It appeared simple enough. No false bottom, side, or lid was perceptible. Next he introduced his son, a handsome little fellow about ten years old. The boy was

34

enveloped in a net which I myself examined, tied firmly round the
ends, and sealed the knots with my own seal. The boy was slung like
a rabbit in a net and I swung him myself off the ground. Thus
enclosed, the boy was put in the basket. A cloth was borrowed from
an adjacent native and spread over the basket, and the lid then put
over the whole. The juggler then went through some other antics,
but I did not take my eye from the basket. After a very short time
the man removed the lid, took a leap into the air and came down
with all his weight, right in the centre of the basket. Had
the boy been there, the shock was enough to rupture his diaphragm,
we only heard a groan. Again the lid was put on the basket. The
juggler took a sharp long slender rapier like sword, and ran it through
and through the basket. Blood issued freely. The natives looked
horror stricken and gasped out their cries of pity. I must confess I
was puzzled. I was still more dumbfounded when the juggler
began to call out loudly in Hindoostanee for his boy. A childish
voice *seemingly from a great distance* answered him. The call and the
answer was repeated, this time little a nearer, until at length the boy
smiling and uninjured, came tripping through the crowd from the
entaiae of the verandah. The basket was opened and there at the
bottom, lay the *empty* net, seals intact, and not a tittle of evidence to
show how the trick was done.

Now surely you will admit that this was more wonderful than
any of the so called spirit manifestations that the most gifted medium
has ever received. Every sense was deceived, and yet the explanation
to those who know the trick is very simple. The spirits have nothing
to do with it. I might go on to describe the mango tricks and other
equally wonderful and equally capable of explanation, but space
forbids.

Some people make a great point of having taken different coloured
pencils to Slade's seances. One gentleman took a green pencil, which
was put upon one corner of the slate and the writing was green—
ergo. the spirits must have written with it, because Dr. Slade could
not have known what colour the pencil was, and he denied having
written the message. A most convincing test indeed. The same
gentleman is not, however, satisfied. He wishes to have a *séance,*
during which one of the company (let us hope a candid sceptic)
will lie beneath the table. That seems fair. I have seen a
common village juggler in India mix five or six different coloured
powders together, put them into a tumbler full of water, and drink
them off. I have examined his mouth to see that the powders were
not concealed there. Then with his hands tied behind his back, I
have asked him to produce a yellow powder. He grates his teeth and
out comes a pile of DRY yellow powder on the top of his little drum
Ask for blue, the blue is produced. Ask for white, the white succeeds
the blue, and so on, whatever colour you name, that colour instantly
appears. Surely this is more wonderful than all the knocking and
tapping and vague answers to leading questions, and deflections of the
compass, which anyone can cause by manipulating a piece of iron
under the table with their feet or hands, or by other mechanical

means. And so with all the other exceedingly commonplace phenomena of spirit mediums which credulity invests with a supernatural character, and which in not one solitary instance have been found to stand the rigid scrutiny of a calm unbiassed scientific investigation.

Some fond loving grieving impressionable one, is perhaps crushed beneath the staggering blow of some sudden bereavement. Oh he thinks if I could but hear the loved one's voice once more. If I could only get a loving tender forgiving message. If I only knew my lost one was happy. The professional medium takes advantage of this state of feeling, professes to satisfy the yearning of bereaved affection, and for money—"no dollar, no show"—sports with this sacred feeling, desecrates the sanctuary of grief; juggles with the most tender and sacred sentiments of humanity, and out of the purest and tenderest throbbings of a wounded heart's deep emotion, forges the most iniquitous and pernicious fraud that ever assumed the sacred name of religion. Oh it is a shame—what a vile atrocious libel on the immortality of the soul—what a ghastly parody on the beatitude of eternal union with our Creator after death. Is this the "liberty of the children of God" "wherewith he makes us free?" Mourner, wouldst thou not rather believe that thine honoured and lamented dead, was with the angels before God's throne, mingling their hallelujahs with the eternal choir, than in a state of constant thraldom and subjection, at the beck and call of every knavish mercenary wretch, who for the sake of a miserable coin, pretends to call them from their sphere of glory, from the presence of the God of the whole earth, to do what? To rattle amongst a few ricketty chairs and tables or give inane maundering ungrammatical answers on a slate, to questions propounded by ignorance, presumption, cupidity, or curiosity.

This, I am aware, is not scientific argument. It is sentimental. There are some more easily touched by sentiment than by scientific demonstration. I only want to expose an unhallowed nefarious fraud, and I do not like to see gentle loving natures despoiled and deluded by scheming tricksters.

If these spiritualistic mediums court the fullest investigation, as they say they do, why is it that they advance the hypothesis that doubt defeats elucidation? Why are the phenomena confined to those places and occasions only, when the medium can do as he pleases in the disposition of his paraphernalia; can dictate his own terms as to the method of enquiry; can claim only those points that tell in favour of his own assertions, assumptions or pretensions, and repudiate every thing unfavourable contradictory or antagonistic, can under the most favourable circumstances only achieve the baldest and most barren results, and in face of detection and exposure take refuge in the most barefaced subterfuge and brazen effrontery of denial. These are questions which the "candid sceptic" may surely require answered before he is asked to swallow the mass of crude transcendental rubbish, the pseudo-German mysticism, the false physiology, and spurious psychology that go to make up the religion of spiritualism. There is not a practised speaker at our bar or in our pulpits, who will not preach us eloquently as logically and as lengthily, as any trance lecturer who ever assumed to embody the thoughts and opinions of the most illustrious defunct orator, be he John Stewart or Demosthenes. Thomas Walker was in my opinion a most third rate speaker. Dr. Beg thoroughly exposed his ignorance and blasphemy, yet are there hundreds in Sydney who believe him to have been all he asserted himself to be. Thomas with all his spiritualism had a most material regard for the nimble shilling, and when the coin no longer flowed into the treasury, he took his sleepy orations elsewhere. I hear he is back again. Will some shorthand reporter report him *verbatim et literatim*, and show the hollow nature of his pretensions?

One very heavenly characteristic of the spirits noticed by professional mediums is their great obligingness as a rule. The answer *expected* is generally the answer received. A friend of mine in Calcutta being at the seance of a professional biologist and medium called up the spirits of Shylock and Falstaff. This was proof positive that Shakespearean characters were all drawn from the life, and my friend's estimate of Shakespeare's genius sunk somewhat. He was somewhat reassured however to find Shakespeare sinning in such good company as Charles Dickens, for on wishing a message from the immortal Mrs. Arris, Sairey Gamp's apochryphal friend, a message was straightway received from that mythical lady. This is not one bit more absurd than the experiences of a certain very elevated and refined spiritualist circle in Sydney. The manifestations in this favoured circle are generally from titled relatives, the very rank of the dead being thus made to pander to the vanity of the living, but more than this, they have embodied or materialised an abstract idea which under the guise of the spirit of Purity, rattles the chairs and tables about much to the comfort and delectation doubtless of these egregiously self deluded investigators after truth. Could the force of humbug farther go? In marked contrast with this pure circle we have another so shadowed by the dire and baleful influences of evil spirits that a very well known gifted spiritualist writer, lecturer and medium, on a recent occasion on entering a judge's room was seized with excessive tremors and had fairly to bolt from the private sanctuary of this representative of Rhadamanthus, owing as she said to the abnormal prevalence of evil spirits in the room. It is such fustian as this that common sense Christians are required to found a new religion upon.

What wonder with so many gulls and pigeons to be plucked that hawks and vultures abound. Next to religious aberrations, hypochondria and monomania affect the medical atmosphere. After nostrums to "minister to a mind diseased" to heal the ailments of the soul, come quackeries and empiricism for the "ills that flesh is heir to"—Slade, Madame Von Halle, the well known New York notoriety, Clara Antonio and others, affect the treatment of mental ailments. They (Walker and others) bring healing to the weary longing soul, from the realms of spirit land. There are others who as the spirits in the most impudent empiricism and who number their dupes by hundreds. Not a medical man in this town but could give scores of cases where simple people have been ruined in health, reputation, pocket, and peace of mind, by these rapacious mediumistic quacks. There was a Miss Armstrong for instance from Melbourne, another burning and shining light among the spiritualists, whose modest fee is from a guinea to half-a-guinea for a prescription, and who claims to be the medium of a deceased Indian herbalist, Dr. Pierce. She had hundreds of clients in Sydney. Feeling the pulse of the patient she gives a snort and a kick as Walker used to do, closes her eyes and in a shaky character writes out a prescription which a little diligent search might discover in any old housewifes book of recipes. Mr. Cole was another of this class. Who then can wonder that when fools were so plentiful and so lavish with their fees, that the Heathen Chinee with the precocity which is so characteristic of the followers of Confucius, should not make an endeavour to intercept a few drops of the golden shower.

A Chinaman accordingly we find setting up shop with a convenient theory of his own. He pretends to be able to see through the human body. The principles of his medical practice are charmingly simple. All disease is just so many clots of blood in your "innards." These his medicines profess to remove. He draws a diagram in Chinese. I have seen several of them myself. Makes up a compound of some abominable filth, and so also is growing rich from the fees which credulous fools are found willing to give him. The Chinese doctor is, like Slade, a cute observer, quick in an emergency, and a clever student of character. A patient went into his place the other day who had a habit of twisting his whisker and putting the end in his mouth. Sing Song, as we shall call the Heathen Esculapius, twigged this peculiarity in a moment. Giving the hypochondriac a sounding slap on the stomach which made him jump, he said: "Ah, you welly bad. I know what the matter with you. You chew whisker. You got ball hair youl tomack. Al right. I culee you." His rapid action disconcerted the patient. Before he had time to think the pig-tailed Galen had administered a strong purgative. He prepared a ball of hair from the stripping of an old chair, and ere the patient left the premises he made him believe that his medicine had relieved him of a ball of horse hair. This is a fact. And yet we wonder at spiritualism making converts and gaining adherents in the face of such Brobdignagian credulity as this. Another well-known sporting character of Bathurst thus details his experience of the Chinese doctor's diagnosis:—"He came up and slapped me on the breast," said he, "looked at me through a bloomin' a y-glass sort of thing, shook his head—said 'You welly bad.' Then began to count on his fingers. Said, 'You welly bad—awful bad. You welly bad with wind. No can live long. You live one, two, three, four, five, six, seven years and three months.'" The old sport when he got thus far said: "The bloomin' three months cooked me and I left!"

Now this reads very funny, but it has its sad and serious side. Worse than the men of ancient Athens, hundreds of us are drifting from all anchorage, abandoning all faith in God, eagerly seeking "something new" to satisfy the morbid craving for religious excitement and new spiritual experience. They will not let their common sense speak. It has been PROVED that professed mediums do many of their seemingly mysterious manifestations by jugglery. If they employ trickery in one part of their performance, and claim that the spirits of the dead are doing what they have been detected in doing, is it not fair reasoning by analogy that their answers and other manifestations are also the result of trickery and imposture. We hear: "Oh, but how could he have known so-and-so? How could he have answered such-and-such?" All these stories utterly collapse before calm analysis. They are only privileged to receive messages who are prepared unhesitatingly and fully to credit and believe the medium. They are consequently biassed observers. In every case I have yet heard recorded pitiable self-deception is present. Exaggeration—often unconscious—is apparent, and even, with all this, the manifestations under the most favourable circumstances, are clumsy, imperfect, unprogressive, unsatisfying, monotypical. redolent of trickery and jugglery, an insult to our spiritual natures and a libel on our common sense. None the less are they dangerous and disquieting. They fascinate many weak-minded people. They unsettle the judgment of the facile and timid. They are edged tools in the hands of unscrupulous knaves, and they should be reprobated, exposed, and denounced by every honest lover of truth.

There is no need to run after mediums, if the spirits can tell us no more than the cleverest medium has yet elicited from them. The deflection of a compass needle, the imitation of a dead friend's handwriting, however cleverly imitated, is a poor exchange for humble trust in God. All the knockings, and scratchings, and rappings, of the most successful seance, seem mean and pitiful, beside the smallest revelation of God's infinite power and goodness in the humblest of his works. If you wish to pry into the unknown, to fathom the mysterious, to unravel the puzzling problems of mental and physical being, to unveil the future, and look into the great "beyond"—slate scratchings, table rappings, planchette writings, and all the tinsel and tag-rag and flimsy frauds of the cleverest medium that ever lived, will not advance you a scintilla of the distance, which one hour's silent prayerful communion with Nature and your own thoughts will give you.. "The beginning of knowledge is the fear of God," and a much better and more spiritual authority than Thomas Walker or Dr. Slade has written.

"In the multitude of dreams and many words, there are also divers vanities; BUT FEAR THOU GOD."

"MAORI."

SPIRITUALISM CONSIDERED AS AN INFECTIOUS MENTAL DISEASE.

———o———

In 1876, the Physical Society of St. Petersburg nominated a Commission to examine into the phenomena of Spiritualism. After a prolonged and impartial inquiry, the conclusion arrived at was, " that those so-called spiritual manifestations proceed from unconscious movements, or from conscious imposture, and the spiritual doctrine is a superstition."

Later, in the same year, Dr. W. B. Carpenter, in a lecture on Spiritualism, delivered at the London Institution, insisted that in the inquiry into the so-called phenomena and facts of Spiritualism, nobody was to be trusted ; that almost everything in it must be the result of either deception, or self-deception, and that there was an immense difference between the fact itself, and the observer's idea of the fact. In conclusion, he said, that these investigations and practices were calculated to produce insanity, because insanity was nothing more than the possession of a " fixed idea " which tinctured everything with which we had to deal.

Following out the ideas suggested by the Physical Society of St. Petersburg and Dr Carpenter, it is my intention to enter into an analytical investigation of certain phenomena, associated with Spiritualism, and place the result in a light heretofore either overlooked or ignored, before the public, many of whom have hitherto appeared incapable of judging these so-called phenomena by any logical process.

Notwithstanding the assumption that a healthy brain is an essential condition upon which depends the normal state of the human mind in its full vigour, there are many and various conditions of the brain and nerves capable of producing certain results upon the mind which we reckon as manifestations of disorder, aberration, and disease, the many phases of which bridge over the gap that intervenes between rationality and insanity. Several wonderful examples of unnatural and morbid states are known to the medical profession under the heads of hysteria, hypochondriasis, catalepsy, ecstasy, and trance, to which may be added the curious conditions known as double consciousness, and somnambulism, or sleep-walking : any of which various conditions may not only occur during the progress of some well-known malady, but sometimes happen spontaneously without a known cause, or in consequence of powerful emotions. It also is sometimes possible (and, indeed, to the exclusion of all deception) to induce them artificially. As is known, this may be accomplished in perfectly healthy people, but, nevertheless, more frequently in nervous and especially in hysterical people, by various manipulations. It appears to be a point in all contrivances undertaken for this purpose, to fix the attention on one object, or to direct the attention very steadfastly in one direction. The condition is most frequently induced by the subjects directing their eyes fixedly upon a dazzling object: sometimes it may be called forth by one placing the fingers for sometime upon the eyeballs, or by spreading a cloth over the head of the patient. It may sometimes be produced by passing the hand over the skin, or by various mysterious gestures which arrest the attention of the patients, or finally by a determination of the latter to subjugate themselves to certain ideas. On some animals also, it is well-known, one might induce quite a similar condition by keeping their bodies fixed for some time, or by holding dazzling objects to their eyes.

This is simply a scientific explanation of the condition popularly known as mesmerism; which is, in other words, an hysterical condition artificially induced. To be a suitable subject for mesmerism implies an individual of an hysterical tendency.

Spiritualists acknowledge that spiritualism and mesmerism differ only in one respect: namely, that in the former a mortal is operated upon by a disembodied spirit, whereas in the latter one mortal is subjected to the will of another mortal.

There are very many forms of unconscious hysteria, and slight mental aberration, which we daily witness without thinking of, or even recognising them. For example, the propagation of a yawn, the irresistible slumber under the drone of a dull preacher, or the unconscious imitation of certain peculiarities of an individual with whom we may be continually thrown into contact. A very familiar form of hysterical illusion occurs in the case of a young mother, who deems her offspring to be the most beautiful and amiable creature in existence, notwithstanding the very frequent fact of its being the very opposite.

From these very slight disturbances of the natural harmony and equilibrium of the human mind, from a state of perfect health, there is possible, a gradual deflection to varying conditions of disease, graduating imperceptibly from the main road of common sense into the byroads of peculiarity, eccentricity, derangement, aberration, and incipient madness, finally terminating in the broad and terrible thoroughfare of permanent insanity.

In hysteria, acting as it does upon the most subtle instincts of the human mind, do we find the groundwork for modern spiritualism. This is the mysterious something so inexplicable that at first fascinates, and then awes the unscientific inquirer into the subject. Add to certain natural phenomena, hysterical influences, credulity, deception, human gullibility, and cruel imposture, then behold before you the ghostly structure of the latest human craze—Spiritualism, a highly infectious mental disease !

The object of this paper is to clearly and distinctly point out the extent of natural psychical phenomena associated with this subject, to define where it terminates, and where self-deception and culpable imposture becomes incorporated with, and superadded to, it. Truly the most insidious kind of deception is that in which truth and falsehood are skilfully interwoven.

Independent of a hysterical condition there are certain processes by which ideas become associated in our minds by habit or otherwise, and one idea being awakened, brings another or others, thus forming a train of thought ; this arising as it does within us, is termed the process of *internal* suggestion. Impressions coming from without originate or modify these trains constituting what is termed *external* suggestion. While awake and in a normal condition, the *will* interferes with and directs these trains of thought, selecting some ideas to be dwelt upon, and comparing them with others and present impressions. Now, in the various phases of an hysterical condition the *will* and with it the *judgment* seem completely suspended ; and under its own internal suggestions the mind becomes a mere automaton, while external suggestions, if they act at all, act as though upon a machine. Again, it is known to psychists that the effect of concentrated attention on any object of thought has the effect of intensifying the impression received. This may proceed so far, in morbid states of the nervous system that an idea or revived sensation assumes the vividness of a present impression, and overpowers the evidence of the senses. Ideas thus become *dominant*, over-riding the impressions of the outer world, and carrying themselves into action independently of the will, and even *without the consciousness* of the individual. These dominant ideas play a greater part in human actions and beliefs than is generally known. ' Expectant attention ' acts powerfully upon the bodily organs, and often makes the individual see and hear what he expects to see and hear, and, without his consciousness moves his muscles to bring it about. These are recognised facts in the sciences of physiology and psychology.

Now concerning the manifestations connected with table turning as practised at seances ; Such of them as are genuine, can be explained by the induced hysterical condition, and our acquired knowledge of ' expectant attention.' The inquirers are seated round a table, being impressed with the idea that it may or will move, the *direction* of the expected movement being also agreed upon. Accordingly if none of the party being are sceptical, it generally does move after a time, all declaring in perfect good faith that they did not press. Faraday however proved by a very clever contrivance, that there always is a pressure, though without the will or consciousness of the performers, and this is only what is to be looked for, from the voluntary effects of a dominant idea. So far we have a scientific and rational explanation. The same applies to table rapping in which by certain oscillations, the table knocks with one or other of its legs upon the floor, and by a preconcerted code of signals answers questions. True, this explanation does not by itself suffice for many of the wonders *related* by believers to have happened. But all such are to be received with suspicion, and that without accusing the relaters of bad faith.

This is the point in table turning and spirit rapping where natural phenomena ends, and unconscious deception begins. The very disposition to look for something out of the usual course makes the inquirers incapable for the time, of distinguishing what actually happens from what they expect to happen. The agency of the *expectant ideas* of the performers in these cases is apparent in their own narratives. Would it not be strange that spirits should reveal heaven to Robert Owen otherwise than as organised on his own social theory, while a protestant clergyman finds the world of spirits pervaded by a horror of the pope, and to pious Scotch Presbyterians, every revelation regarding it is completely in accord with the Calvinistic theory?

The operation of the planchette in its mystic writings can now be understood, the peculiar function of writing by its means is one that by some is easily acquired, by others it requires a long devotion and continued practice before the requisite mental abstraction can be attained to induce the necessary automatic action of the hand, unconsciously controlled by the mind and guided by unsuspected hopes, and aspirations. The result of my own observation is that the greater the hysterical tendency of the subject, the more easily is the habit acquired.

The next, and certainly a more serious symptom of this strange malady to be considered, is the subject of trance-speaking. As a means of elucidating the subject in a medical aspect, I shall quote the words of the most recent medical authority, as well as other writers, upon a certain modification of hysteria * :—" Finally, as regards the attacks of *somnambulism, sleep-walking, wakefulness, magnetic sleep, hypnotism,* and *ecstasy,* and whatever else those attacks have been named, which are met with in the hysterical, they are merely varieties of the form of catalepsy known as *hysterical trance.* We have always in such cases to deal with dreamy conditions. When thus affected, patients can, actuated by the promptings of their dream, execute various complicated movements, when, like animals, whose brains have been removed, without noting their surroundings, they are guided by stimuli affecting the senses, cleverly avoid obstructions, and under the most dangerous circumstances preserve their corporeal equilibrium. Sometimes they answer particular questions addressed to them, in a perfectly rational manner : in these answers the influence of the revelations of their dream is frequently to be recognised. Moreover, as the sensory apprehension, as already mentioned, is occasionally quickened, so apparently wonderful powers of distinguishing objects and persons by means of different senses are observed. One must, however, be very sceptical in testing such statements. For, on the one hand, there frequently exists in the patients themselves, who suffer from such attacks, a tendency to exaggeration and deceit ; and, on the other hand, they are easily misled by their friends, who are either themselves superstitious, or trade upon the superstition of others. The peculiar conditions are then ascribed to a supernatural or divine influence, and in order to render the pretended wonder still more wonderful, it is embellished with all manner of falsehood."

Abercrombie† states that there is a remarkable peculiarity in many cases of mental aberration. inducing great activity of mind and

* Ziemssen's Cyclopedia of Practice of Medicine, Vol. XIV., page 534.
† Abercrombie's Intellectual Powers, p. 243

rapidity of conception, a tendency to seize rapidly upon incidental or partial relations of things, and often a fertility of imagination, which changes the character of the mind, sometimes without remarkably disturbing it. The memory in such cases is entire, or even appears more ready than in health : and old associations are called up with a rapidity quite unknown to the individual in his sound state of mind. One gentleman is mentioned who enjoyed his paroxysms with pleasure. He said : " Everything appeared easy to me. No obstacles presented themselves either in theory or in practice. My memory acquired all of a sudden a singular degree of perfection. Long passages of Latin authors occurred to my mind. In general, I have great difficulty in finding rhythmical terminations, but then I could write verses with as great facility as prose."

Dr. Copeland mentions a curious fact in connection with this subject. He says that many of the Italian Improvisatori are in possession of their peculiar faculty only when they are in a state of ecstatic trance ; and that few of them enjoy good health, or consider their gifts as otherwise than something morbid.

Sir Thomas Watson quaintly remarks : "I take it for granted that they who were in the habit of speaking, a few years since, in some of our places of worship, in what they called *unknown tongues*, were either gross impostors who deserved to be whipped, or persons labouring under this disease and wanting physic."

I need not prolong this paper by adducing further authorities, examples, or illustrations in order to identify well-known diseased conditions of the human mind with modern so-called spiritual trance speaking. The symptoms of both are exactly the same, in no instance does the victim of the malady exhibit a capacity beyond his possible ability, of course, making allowances for the mysterious influence of his temporarily diseased brain, which is capable of inducing sublime hallucinations, visions, and soul-inspiring dreams ; the senses abnormally quickened, the mind revived and re-enriched by the renewed impressions of long-forgotten scenes, often the memory of languages, learnt, but since forgotten, is revived. To the surprise of those present, volubility of tongue and elocution, which in ordinary life the patient was deemed incapable of producing are now exhibited.

For the benefit of those who may not have witnessed a trance speaking seance, I shall out line the proceedings I witnessed on such an occasion in Sydney a short time ago. The medium on this occasion was a quiet looking, delicate, nervous, excitable gentleman, for whom I entertain the highest respect. I fully believed him when he assured me that he was perfectly insensible during his trance condition. I have since written to the husband of the amiable lady of the house, assuring him it never for one moment entered my mind that any wilful deception or collusion was practised on the occasion. The room having been partially darkened, we assembled round the table, and placed our hands in the usual manner ; I watched the medium closely, to me he was a physiological study. The usual gyrations and rockings of the table having commenced, nervous twitchings of his hands and arms ushered in the hysterical attack. The eyelids became tremulous, the features worked and perspiration began to ooze from every pore. He broke the circle by spasmodically rising up. He called out a name, I think it was Paoton. He jerked out some unintelligible gibberish. I was now informed that he was in a spiritual trance and controlled by an Indian Chief, he who was speaking through him in his native dialect. I must acknowledge that he acted the savage's part to life. In a short period certainly shorter than an hour he personated various individuals among them an organ blower, a musician, an exponent of mesmerism, and Lord Brougham. While under the musician's influence he strummed upon a piano, not unharmoniously, yet not musically, there were rhythm and chords, yet no music, plenty of sound, no execution. During the fit, for it was a well marked fit of hysteria, this gentleman was at times totally insensible to pain for I pinched him several times, and he did not wince. The pupils of the eyes were dilated, the eyes extremely sensitive to light. At one time he became so exhausted by his physical exertions that by an effort of will he stopped the proceedings and took a rest, after which he with a surprising facility resumed his fit and impersonations. During the whole of this phenomena he displayed no capacity beyond what I took to be his ordinary abilities. Lord Brougham's speech was very mediocre for such an eminent statesman. Yet the spiritual believing portion of the audience by whom I was surrounded, not knowing any reasonable explanation for what they saw and heard, attributed it to spiritualistic influence. Their logic was on a par with that of the blackfellow in a cave, who hearing a voice that he could not explain, exclaimed "Debble, Debble, he jump out of the rock!"

From the result of my own observation and the admissions of spiritualists themselves, it appears that many of the erroneous beliefs connected with spiritualism are not only fostered but progressively developed by education and practice. This brings me to the highest stage of spiritualistic perfection, in which the disease leads to a deception of the senses: namely, materialisation.

It takes a considerable time to educate oneself to that condition in which *true visionary hallucinations* are produced, such as are often associated with ecstasy. A spiritualist told me that it takes persistent sittings in a darkened room for two or more years before materialisation, or the property of seeing spirits as though in the flesh, can be attained. Somewhat antecedent to this stage, excitations and aberrations of the senses of hearing and seeing are induced. While worked up to a certain pitch of hysterical ecstasy, subjects become aware of events frequently unobserved by the healthy, and a greater acuteness of hearing may be artificially induced by the avoidance of all possible sounds. But there occur also cases of actual exaggeration and perversion of these faculties in consequence of the progress of the disease. Thus the subjects frequently think they hear the ringing of bells, blowing of horns, and so forth. True hallucinations of hearing are suggested by external impressions. Thus the senseless strumming on a piano appears to be most heavenly music. Sounds like a band playing have been heard inside a piano, the keys of which remain untouched. An eccentricity of vision also induced is that heavy inanimate objects, such as pianos, beds, and tables appear to dance, jump, and follow the deluded victim about the room. These are serious symptoms of the disease, and frequently constitute that transition which leads to definite mental aberration.

Hitherto I have limited myself to the description of certain natural phenomena and delusions of the human mind leading up to certain results, and to an induced diseased condition combined with 'these results; added to which are various misinterpretations and misconceptions consequent upon the inability of certain individuals to grasp the whole subject so as to elucidate clearly the result of a natural process from the fallacy superadded thereto. To ordinary minds, especially such as are not educated to logical processes of reasoning, this chaotic combination is very puzzling, and tends to keep the reason confused and poised in an unbalanced state of uncertainty. Thus have we multitudes standing upon the brink of spiritualism—unhappy, doubting, and perplexed. At this juncture comes into play the element that I cannot otherwise stigmatise than as cruel imposture. I allude to the malpractices of professional mediums, who by a series of cleverly contrived illusions, so manage to mystify, delude, and lead them for ever into that track which robs them of their Christianity, leads up to atheism, and terminates in insanity.

SAMUEL T. KNAGGS, M.D., F.R.C.S. &c., &c.

Newcastle.

"THE SPIRITS" AT ALBURY.

———o———

Tʜᴇ following interesting account of the doings of Dr. Slade and the Spirits on the Border is taken from the *Albury Banner* of January 11th. An amusing fact to be noticed herein is that whether in the Riverina, in Sydney, or in Germany, the Spirits are unable to spell their favourite word "investigation." The lithograph of the slate writing in Berlin, mentioned in the article "The World of Dupes" shows that there, as in Australia, they always write "*envestigation*." Really Dr. Slade should take a few lessons in orthography! The *Albury Banner* deserves great credit for its fearless exposure of the medium's tricks. Had the metropolitan journals possessed the same amount of public spirit this "fraud" might not have found so many dupes.

＊　　＊　　＊　　＊　　＊　　＊

Iɴ compliance with a polite invitation from Dr. Slade, a reporter from this journal was present at a private *seance*, attended only by representatives of the press, held at the Globe Hotel. Dr. Slade at the commencement of the *seance* intimated that he only desired those who witnessed the phenomena to describe what they actually saw; and our reporter, acting upon this hint, has endeavoured to narrate as clearly as possible what came under his observation. His narrative is as follows:—" I went into the room and found Dr. Slade had been obliged to send over to Mr. F. A. Selle's for a table. There was a table in the room, but it was not apparently the right article for the spirits to operate upon ; more particularly in the slate-writing demonstration, which requires a certain amount of flat surface under the leaf of the table free from beading or any other obstruction, so that the slate, being pressed against the under part of the leaf, may move about freely. Besides Dr. Slade and myself, there were three other gentlemen present, and under instructions from the medium we all joined hands to ' complete the circle.' I should state that of the four visitors, one only was understood to be a believer in the reality of spiritual manifestations. The other three were connected with the Press, and therefore not prepared to take anything upon trust, but as a matter of course unprejudiced and impartial recorders of facts.

After we had sat watching our hands for a few minutes, the medium asked, 'Do you feel it?' The gentleman who had a leaning towards spiritualism said he did feel the electric current quite plainly. For my part I felt nothing of the kind, nor did the other two gentlemen. Dr. Slade, however, said that he felt it very strongly, and he several times snatched his hands up from the table as if he had received a galvanic shock. Presently there was a very perceptible vibration of the table,—a kind of rapid rocking motion. There was no mistaking this movement, which was obvious to the most sceptical observer. It was produced by spirits. That is to say, if the spirits did not do it Dr. Slade did. Dr. Slade told us he did not do it, *ergo* the spirits did. It is my business to record facts, therefore I mention this quite candidly.

There were, however, two other facts which it may be as well to refer to also. In the first place, the vibrating movement could easily have been produced by any one of the party who chose to press with his wrists on the table in a peculiar way. Secondly, the motion always ceased when Dr. Slade removed his hands from the table. I state these things merely to afford the public all possible *data* they could desire in the investigation of these phenomena. I am aware they do not account for the vibration, because Dr. Slade says he did not shake the table, and I am sure no other of the party did. But wonderful as was this manifestation, it was a trifle to what followed. A slate having been procured, it was held by the medium just under the flap of the table, and a question was then asked by one of the party as to whether the writer of this was a medium. There was a good deal of flapping about of the slate before the query elicited any response. 'the current' apparently being unusually strong and manifesting a general disposition to twist the slate out of the Dr's hand. Ultimately, however, a faint scratching sound was heard, and on the slate being exposed to view there were the words plainly legible, albeit a trifle 'smudgy,' ' He can be.' These words had been written by the spirits. At least the medium frankly told us all that he did not write them, consequently the inference is obvious that the spirits must. But the mysterious Powers had not half exhausted themselves yet. A double slate, or rather, to be more accurate, two slates, were employed; the one slate being placed on the top of the other, with a small piece of pencil between the two surfaces. Here, again, a reply was vouchsafed after the usual preliminary flapping about caused by the force of the ' current.' The absolute *bona fide* of the medium, and the absence of anything in the shape of trickery, were proved to demonstration by the doctor's giving one of the party a slate to hold himself. It is true that the writing did not then appear, but this was most satisfactorily accounted for by the fact that the person in question was not a medium. After some ten minutes passed in receiving these mysterious messages from the spirit world Dr. Slade inquired of his intangible acquaintances whether they would favor the circle with yet one more manifestation. Quick as thought came the reply in the shape of raps somewhere in the vicinity of the legs of the table. In connection with these raps, which were pronounced by the medium to be a reply in the affirmative, a curious fact came under my notice which proves to my mind that the spirits are not absolutely immaterial. The substance of which they are composed is probably a very subtle ether, ordinarily visible to the human eye, but still, under some conditions, opaque. And the way that I arrived at the conclusion was in this wise. When the knocks came under the table I chanced to be looking on the floor of the room. The medium sat between me and the window, and I could not see his feet, but simultaneously with each rap I saw a shadow pass rapidly over the floor, as though some substance had been moved quickly at the moment that each knock was given. I mention this in order that nothing, even of the most trivial character, may be lost to the public with regard to this very interesting séance. Of course the shadow I saw was not the shadow of Dr. Slade's feet, because he told me the knocks were not made by him; the circumstance is, however, interesting as opening up in connection with these remarkable phenomena a new field of psychological inquiry. The crowning manifestation of the sitting was the sudden raising of the table to a height of eight or ten inches from the floor, Dr. Slade's feet the while being seemingly placed under mine. I say "seemingly" because I know some sceptics would aver that the medium slipped his feet out of his shoes, and that it was only the Dr.'s oxonians upon which I maintained a firm pressure in the interests of science. But Dr. Slade told us all that he did not move the table, so the question as to the whereabouts of his feet lapses after all into insignificance.

I paid Dr. Slade another visit in company with two of the party present on the preceding day. The manifestations were of pretty much the same character as those witnessed previously, but perhaps a little more fully developed. The slate-writings, for example, were more lengthy. And in reference to these writings I noted two fresh facts — the one corroborative of the theory I have before propounded as to the materiality of the Powers, the other affording a singular proof of their lack of elementary education. The first fact was this—Whilst the medium held up the slate on the table for us to hear the scratching sound caused by the Invisibles when at work, the light from the window threw the shadow of a finger—a fat finger—on the table, and this shadow could plainly be seen through a crack between the slate and the table. Fact the second — In one of the letters written by the spirits occurred the word ' investigation '—these illiterate spirits spelt it ' envestigation.' It occurred to me that the medium also, after long converse with these parties, might be demoralised in his orthography. I therefore asked him if he would kindly write one of the sentences given by the spirits at my dictation. He consented, and I chose the passage containing the ill-used pollysyllable, which, sure enough, Dr. Slade wrote out as ' envestigation.' This struck me as such an extraordinary coincidence, that the subsequent manifestations, including as they did a performance upon an accordion, ending with an acrobatic feat by that instrument, failed to arouse in me any further feelings of awe or even of astonishment. To speak seriously, there was not

much in the whole exhibition to excite either feeling in the mind of
any person possessed of ordinary common sense, and not previously
imbued with faith in the manifestations. From beginning to end very
little was done that the very clumsiest of professional conjurors could
not easily have performed! and any little mystery connected with the
slate performance (certainly the cleverest item on the list) could easily
be accounted for if I were to assume that the medium possessed a
tithe of the dexterity in sleight-of-hand displayed by every 'three-
card-man' on a racecourse." Thus, our reporter. We had purposed
appending a few words of comment to his "plain, unvarnished story,"
but on second thoughts we incline to the belief that comment is
unnecessary.

www.ingramcontent.com/pod-product-compliance
Lightning Source LLC
Chambersburg PA
CBHW021644270326

41931CB00008B/1168